SPIRITS OF THE YULETIDE

A MEDIUM'S GUIDE TO EMBRACING THE MYSTICAL SIDE OF THE HOLIDAYS

RICHARD MOSCHELLA

BEYOND
THE FRAY PUBLISHING

ISBN: 979-8-89234-124-0

Beyond The Fray Publishing,
a division of Beyond The Fray, LLC
San Diego, CA

BEYOND
THE FRAY PUBLISHING

SINCE 2010

CONTENTS

Introduction   vii

1. Origins and Folklore   1
2. A Medium's Perspective   17
3. Channeled Messages From The Fulcrum   49
4. Signs   59
5. Spirits Message   71
6. Yuletide Symbolism and Ritual   87
7. Family Recipes & The Spirit of Saint Nicholas   99

Afterword   111
About the Author   113
Also by Richard Moschella   115

DEDICATION

I like to dedicate this book to two very special Aunts that made the season memorable and who we miss dearly. Mary Toohey, you made the Christmas season incredibly special and brought our family together. May you always lead us in song and be near, with a wooden spoon in hand.

We love you Aunt Mary

This book is also dedicated with great love to Phyllis Buonauro.

When I think back on so many childhood Christmas memories,
so many of them happened in Aunt Philly's home. You
welcomed the entire family and showed us all the true meaning
of Christmas, in the spirit of Saint Nicholas your generosity
and love were always the most precious gift any child or adult
could receive.

INTRODUCTION

There'll be parties for hosting
Marshmallows for toasting
And caroling out in the snow
There'll be scary ghost stories
And tales of the glories of
Christmases long, long ago

- Eddie Pola / George Wyle

Yule was believed to be the time when the spirits of the dead were passed on to the Otherworld to move on from the living world and to continue their afterlife there. These spirits were honored and celebrated

It's a warm July morning and I'm vacationing with my family on Cape Cod, Massachusetts. We usually try to stay in the Dennis area on the cape because of a beautiful beach on the bayside called Mayflower Beach. This has become our favorite beach for our young children because being on the bay side, there really are no big waves and the kids enjoy the sandbars on low tide. I had just submitted my latest book to my publisher and was starting to book press opportunities for *Only A Thought Away*. Sitting on the beach and sending off a few emails that pertained to upcoming podcasts and interviews, the warm July sun was beating down. The ocean air with the smell of countless sunscreen scents wafting over to our little spot on the beach, reminded me that it might be time to reply to my own lotion. The sound of children's laughter and the occasional gull squawk, I heard the sound of familiar music drifting in the summer breeze. The songs were timeless and caused me to pause, my mind had a hard time processing the sunscreen smell combined with the opening of the song *Santa Claus Is Coming To Town*. Scanning the beach, I noticed the music was coming from a beach tent not too far from where we chose to set up. I found this to be really great, my kids thought it was very cool too.

Realizing we were just about halfway to the Christmas season, I knew why these songs were on today's beach playlist. They were celebrating Christmas in July on the beach today. You haven't lived until you hear White Christmas on a warm sunny beach under the Cape Cod sun. The songs transported me to family celebrations many years ago and made me think of relatives that now are only with us in spirit. Memories of gathering around the piano and singing songs and the endless food that would be at the center of the dining room table. The family coming together, the laughter, the love and the magic of the Christmas season. I quickly grabbed my phone and made a note to myself, *Spirits Of The Yuletide.* Some other topics I jotted down were, what does spirit want us to know about this time of year, the folklore, the ancient connection, ancestors, the symbolism, ritual and coming together to get through the darkest time of year.

Illustration of the Ghost of Christmas Present by John Leech from the 1800s.

I immediately felt that I was on to something and that this might be a project worth pursuing. What I also wanted to get out of this project was a book that could help anyone out there going through a difficult time with a loss of a loved one this time of year. If by reading this book it helps just ease the burden of grief, just a little I feel that it has done its job. This time of year, for many is tremendously happy and tremendously sad all at the same time. We look forward to the younger generations gathering together but we can't help but also look to the past at those no longer at our celebrations that are now in spirit. So, in this book I wanted to encapsulate the ancient connection between the Yuletide and Christmas celebration and how our ancestors are closer than you think during this time of the year. We will also explore the magic of the season and talk about the symbolism and folklore that makes this time of year enchanting. So, let's embark on this journey together and learn about our ancient connection to our ancestors and the celebration of Yule and Christmas. As we enter the darkest time of year, we hold our family close and look forward to another season to come. We gather and sing and make recipes from those long ago. We tell stories and folklore and know the magic that this season brings to young and old. What we also know is that our loved ones are only a thought away and still a part of our celebrations. Our ancestors in spirit are around everyone and everything and we just need to listen and look for the signs. In the end I hope this book will earn a spot on your bookshelf and help you on your journey and perspective of this magical and ancient time of the year. It's a season to embrace the old and look forward to the future and know that the ghosts of Christmas past are closer than you think.

CHAPTER I

ORIGINS AND FOLKLORE

The town is quiet and a blanket of snow covers the ground, the children are nestled and tucked in their beds. Mom and Dad have fallen deep into a winter slumber as the cold wind whips across the rooftop creating a howling that echoes through the wooden walls. The bare trees creak and branches crack as the wind swooshes through the old oak trees. The home is decorated in celebration of the Christmas season and images of a jolly old elf and eight tiny reindeer adorn the walls and living space. In the center of the living room is a beautiful Norway spruce Christmas tree decorated with lights and ornaments. The tree casts an angelic glow of white light into the darkness of the home. On a shelf nearby old photos in picture frames of Christmases long ago offer a glimpse of the past and ancestors that are now only here in spirit. The yuletide is upon us once again and our ancestors on the other side of the veil draw near. We also welcome other yuletide traditions, beings, spirits and monsters that make this time of year magical, meaningful and at times scariest time of the year.

As a medium that communicates with the spirit world I can tell you that our loved ones are always around us. Our connection to those on the other side of the veil is even closer, once a loved one makes the transition into the spirit world. They no longer have to deal with physical distance and now connect with us through energy and consciousness. They are truly only a thought away and still a part of our lives. Through readings for many clients over the years Spirit always shares the importance of family coming together and putting differences aside and celebrating the holidays. It's a time of reflection and embracing traditions of those that have come before us. This honors our ancestors and carries on their legacies to the next generation. In ancient times the winter was a time that would cause dread among the living, fear of not having shelter, food and warmth could be disastrous and bring death to your doorstep. They gathered together and displayed evergreen plants during the winter months to remind themselves that the light and green season would return. The evergreens represented life itself and honored our precious connection to the natural world. Today we cut down Christmas trees and do not realize that we are carrying on an ancient tradition. We sing songs that also have been passed down through generations and also trigger memories of holidays long ago. Then there are the stores that we tell and the gathering around the hearth, as we recount the timeless tales of Charles Dickens and Clement Moore. *A Christmas Carol* is one of the most popular stories and has been made into countless films over the years. At its core it's a ghost story that reminds us that there is good in everyone and it's never too late to make a change. Ghost stories have been a Christmas tradition in England for a long time and have been shared by generations. The tradition of telling ghost stories in the winter predates the Victorian age. It also serves as a reminder to what is at the core of the holiday and the spirit of the season.

"A Visit from St. Nicholas", or also called "The Night Before Christmas" and "'Twas the Night Before Christmas" from its first line, is a poem first published anonymously under the title "Account of a Visit from St. Nicholas" in 1823 and later attributed to Clement Clarke Moore, who claimed authorship in 1837. The poem has been called "arguably the best-known verses ever written by an American" and is largely responsible for some of the conceptions of Santa Claus from the mid-19th century to today. It has had a massive effect on the history of Christmas gift-giving. Before the poem gained wide popularity, American ideas had varied considerably about Saint Nicholas and other Christmastide visitors.

Thomas Nast was a German born American cartoonist and is often considered to be the "father of the American cartoon". It was in 1863 during the American Civil War that Nast Illustrated the cover of Harper's Weekly and gave us one of the first depictions of Santa Claus. The drawing shows Santa distributing presents in a Union Army camp, of course Santa Claus was a Union man.

A second illustration in the magazine showcased a woman praying with young children nestled in their beds and a husband on the battlefront reflecting on his family at home. The illustration is profoundly beautiful but on the top left and right of the drawing is imagery that would add to our mythology of the jolly old elf we call Santa Claus. On the top left you can see Santa and his sleigh on a roof top as he prepares to go down a chimney. Then on the top left of the image we see for the first time, Santa in a magical flying sleigh taking to the sky that's being pulled by reindeer. Nast based Santa's beard and round belly partially on himself and used his wife and children as charters in his illustrations and he infused the rooftops and church spires of his hometown of Morristown, New Jersey in his sketches.

His imagery of Santa would vary year to year, Nast would go on to illustrate thirty three images of Santa Claus for Harper's Weekly. The 1881 image known as "Merry Old Santa Claus" is one of Nast's famous portraits of this idol. Santa is shown in his red suit with pipe in hand, holding toys and ushering in an image that would live on forever.

Harper's Weekly 1863

In 1931 Coca-Cola launched a Christmas advertising campaign that focused on a Santa Claus wearing the corporate colors white and red and offering the good boys and girls a cold coke, with a twinkle in his eye. Throughout generations we have all shared in the wonderment and magic of the Christmas season and all tried to stay on the good list in hopes of waking up on Christmas morning and finding toys left under our tree. Now as we grow older and retrospectively look back at the lore of this beloved time of the year, we can see through the red and white suite and flying sleigh and see a much more ancient connection to the holiday. In Norse mythology Odin traverse's, the night sky during Yule and leads a hunt for spirits of the dead that have been released from their earthly bodies and are delivered to the afterlife. Odin was often depicted as a god with long white beard who rode through the sky on his eight legged horse during Yules great hunt. The comparisons to Santa Claus are strikingly similar, the long and white beard, riding through the sky and the eight reindeers. We can get a sense of how ancient these connections are and appreciate them even more today.

1881 Santa Claus by Thomas Nast

We must go back to the fifth century, over 1,500 years ago. The Yule was first celebrated by Germanic pagans marking the winter solstice. This occurs in the Northern Hemisphere (December 21st - 22nd and June 20th - 21st in the

Southern Hemisphere). This pre Christian festival origi-nated in Scandinavia and blended with other pagan cele-brations, into the Christian celebration of Christmas. Historians have deciphered that Yule starts during the longest and coldest time of the year. After this, the days begin to get longer again. The ancient ancestors would celebrate Yule because the sun was going to start making the days last longer, which meant Earth was preparing to become fertile again; fields would soon be ready to sow, and Earth and its creations would soon be reborn. Yule is celebrated during the year's longest nights when the winter season is halfway over. In north arctic areas, the sun disappears entirely. It only appears again toward the end of winter - at the start of the new season. The return of the sunlight is important to a society of hunters and farmers because food won't be so scarce anymore. Some modern celebrations of Yule attempt to recreate ancient traditions, while others have been adapted or reimagined to suit contemporary personal and religious practices.

The Yule was a time to honor ancient traditions and ritu-als, the Celtic druids would give mistletoe as an offering. Mistletoe could be found growing on oak trees and would be considered a blessing and symbolize life during the Yule. The Celts thought that the sun stood still for twelve days marking the darkest time of the year. These dark days would be made brighter by lighting logs to keep away evil and welcome good fortune, this practice today is observed by lighting the Yule log. As Christianity became more widespread, it adopted certain pagan traditions into its celebrations.

At the core of the celebration of Yule is tradition and honoring our ancestors. This tradition from Pagan to Christianity echoes bringing light to the darkness, hope, celebrating family, honoring our dead, gathering together, looking back and at the same time looking forward to the new year to come. These traditions help the next generation gain a deeper understanding of who they are and where they came from. Through the best of times and the worst of times that connection to family and ancestry is always present. Some historians believe that Yule was a sort of Norse Day of the Dead, while others believe it was simply a new year festival intended to set the tone for the coming months.

The first time the birth of Jesus Christ was attributed to the date December 25 was in the 4th century, according to early Roman history. The Roman Catholic Church chose to mark Jesus' birthday on December 25th, But in fact, no one actually knows the exact date Jesus was born. Some theologians believe that Jesus was born in the spring because shepherds watched over their flocks during the spring season and not in the winter. Scholars have stated that they feel that Jesus's birthday is actually closer to Easter or the Jewish holiday of Passover than it is to Christmas.

Early celebrations of Christmas are thought to have derived from Roman and other European festivals that marked the end of the harvest, and the winter solstice. Some customs from those celebrations that have endured include decorating homes with greenery, giving gifts, singing songs, and eating special foods. The holiday developed further with the legend of St. Nicholas. In his honor, the Feast of St. Nicholas was marked on December 6 and gifts given the night before. The tradition was well established in many European countries by the 12th century. Eventually, because St. Nicholas' Day and Christmas Day are so close together, their traditions generally were combined. Today Christians and non - religious faiths celebrate and take part in some aspect of this ancient celebration to mark the darkest time of the year and to come together and celebrate family. For some we celebrate the birth of Jesus and if we are celebrating it early and the theologians are right, what is the crime in that. Then for others that look at the commercial and magical narrative of a jolly old elf and his eight tiny reindeer that travels to every home across the world on Christmas eve to bring presents to the good boys and girls. I feel that it's ok to celebrate this time of year and incorporate whatever aspects you feel resonates with your family. The Yule and Christmas customs can coexist and bring perspective, ritual and reflection to this season. Giving thanks to the creator and understanding our connotation to the natural world and being grateful for what you have. So, we gather and share food and raise a glass to our ancestors, we celebrate traditions and sing songs that echo through generations.

The Season For Telling Ghost Stories

We know that the Christmas season is a time to come together with family and friends and share stories and songs that are so dear to our childhood. Songs about snowmen and Santa Claus and the famous poem *A Visit From Saint Nicholas*. But little do you know that it's a very old tradition to tell much darker stories this time of year as well. According to Sara Cleto, a folklorist specializing in British literature and co-founder of The Carterhaugh School of Folklore and the Fantastic, the season around winter solstice, has been one of transition and change. "For a very, very, very long time, the season has provoked oral stories about spooky things in many different countries and cultures all over the world," she says.

Telling supernatural tales during the Christmas celebration goes far back to the Victorian era, as families would gather together spooky storytelling provided entertainment on long dark evenings before electricity. "The long midwinter nights meant folks had to stop working early, and they spent their leisure hours huddled close to the fire," says Tara Moore, an assistant professor of English at Elizabethtown College, author of Victorian Christmas in Print, and editor of *The Valancourt Book of Victorian Christmas Ghost Stories*. "Plus, you didn't need to be literate to retell the local ghost story." Some of these tales were passed down from generations and elaborated upon with every retelling. Stories of ghostly apparitions and creatures lurking in the winter darkness or perhaps hiding in the home. This was an old oral tradition for many and once the steam powered printing press was invented during the industrial revolution, these scary ghostly tales could be published and distributed throughout the land. The Victorians commercialized and now could sell these tales of old to the next generation. With higher literacy rates and cheaper printing costs this was the dawn of a new era of storytelling.

One of the most known works of a Christmas ghost story is Charles Dickens 1843 novella *A Christmas Carol*, Dickens played a huge part in popularizing the genre in England and wrote many different Christmas novellas that contained ghosts. But in *A Christmas Carol* struck gold with the story of redemption, reunion and forgiveness that became an immortal tale that according to The Internet Movie Database has been adapted over 100 times for the silver screen. The novella's success in the U.S. likely had more to do with Dickens' existing massive fan base than it did Americans' interest in incorporating the supernatural into Christmas.

> *"I wear the chain I forged in life," replied the Ghost. "I made it link by link, and yard by yard; I girded it on my own free will, and*

of my own free will I wore it.": — Charles Dickens, A Christmas Carol

In fact, in Shakespeare's 1611 play *The Winter's Tale*, Mamillius proclaims "A sad tale's best for winter. I have one of sprites and goblins." Our fascination with what lurks in the darkness goes back to ancient times and through storytelling filled many dark nights next to burning fires with fighting and chilling tales of ghosts and monsters. The Neanderthals painted images on cave walls that told of trials and tribulations of early man over 43,000 years ago. This prehistoric art can help us understand the history of Homo sapiens and how they developed abstract thoughts. Some believe that the paintings were a form of creativity, spirituality, and sentimental thinking. Others have proposed that the paintings were made by shamans who were trying to connect with the spirit world.

We gain a perspective at how far back humans have been gathering together and communicating through storytelling. It seems that it is natural for one to ponder what happens when one exits the earthly plane and goes beyond the veil. The Victorians perfected the art of combining ghostly tales of the supernatural with Christmas and found many of their characters in Yuletide folklore.

Krampus

Half man, half man goat, Krampus is said to have originated in Germany, his name being taken from the German Krampen, meaning claw. Though he is originally said to have been the son of the Norse goddess, Hel, with the spread of Christianity he became associated with Christmas as the counterpart to St Nicholas. He is described as a hairy figure with cloven hooves and sharp horns. Krampus, along with the friendlier St Nicholas are said to visit on 5th December. Where St Nicholas rewards the good children, Krampus is there to punish the bad. He carries with him a wooden switch or in some versions, chains which are used to beat the children who had been naughty. In some stories he may even snatch the unwary child away, stuffing them into his sack and carrying them off to his lair. We can see a modern day interpretation of Krampus's inspiration of Dr Seuss's Grinch.

La Befana

Often characterized as a good witch who gives presents to children on the night of Epiphany January 5th, La Befana is not originally a witch at all though she does ride on a broomstick. An Italian legend tells that La Befana was once an elderly woman who heard a knock on the door. Opening it, she found the three wise men, lost and looking for Bethlehem. Giving them a place to stay for the night, La Befana was told of their quest to follow the star and find the new-born king. They invited her to join them, but La Befana refused, saying she needed to sweep the floor and finish her chores. Shortly after the wise men left La Befana changed her mind, filling a basket with treats and sweets. Though she hurried, she was unable to catch up with the wise men, or to find the infant Jesus. Instead, she leaves treats for the children of the houses she visits while still looking for the holy child.

<u>Grýla</u>

In Icelandic folklore, Grýla is a monstrous entity who lives in the wilderness of Iceland. The name Grýla first appears in medieval history. However, the earliest unambiguous references to Grýla's gender and her association with Christmas date emerges from the seventeenth century. In seventeenth-century poems about Grýla, she is generally represented as a hideous and greedy ogress who wanders between human settlements and demands charity from those she encounters, often asking for naughty children. Modern depictions of Grýla tend to focus more strongly on her role as the mother of her troll sons known as the Yule Lads. Today, the most monstrous aspects of her character and appearance (such as her appetite for children) are generally toned down for younger audiences.

The Yule Cat

The Yule cat is a huge and vicious cat from Icelandic Christmas folklore that is said to lurk in the snowy countryside during the Christmas season and eat people who do not receive new clothing before Christmas. This was used as a threat for farmworkers to finish processing the wool they collected in the autumn before Christmas. Those who got their work done would have new clothing to show for it and be safe from the Yule Cat. So, as you purchase gifts for your loved ones this year, perhaps think about a new shirt or even a pair of socks to keep the Yule Cat at bay.

So, as you gather together with your family, perhaps you might want to tell a ghost story or two during your celebration of this ancient holiday. The tapestry of the Yuletide is incredibly rich with folklore and magic that makes this for many their favorite time of the year. The retelling of ageless stories and recollecting memories from long ago, keep our ancestors alive in all of us. This is the most wonderful time of the year, for just one night we believe that reindeer can fly, a jolly old elf brings presents to the good girls and boys and elves inhabit our homes repointing our behavior back to the North Pole. We have learned about the holiday's origins and have set the stage for our journey beyond the folklore and characters that we have come to know.

As we delve deeper into the spiritual side of the Yuletide and our celebration of Christmas, we will come to find that our loved ones on the other side of the veil have never left us at all. When we think of them and mention their names or tell family stories, that's a direct line to the other side. It's as close we can come to picking up a phone and calling them. We connect with consciousness and that is our divine link to our loved ones in spirit. So, I implore you to talk about your loved ones and tell their stories, not only do you keep their memory alive for future generations, but you also connect directly to them. I like to quote Bruce Springsteen:

> "And the only thing I can guarantee tonight is that if you're here, and we're here, then those that are missing are here with us. If you're here and we're here, then they are here."

CHAPTER 2
A MEDIUM'S PERSPECTIVE

I personally know from readings that I have done that spirit really emphasizes the importance of giving the gift of memories instead of material things. When spirit connects with their loved ones, they share memories of places they have gone and experiences that they shared. These gifts are invaluable and make memories that will be here long after you are gone. We seem to obsess over the monetary value and the hottest trends but in reality that does not matter at all. I have been given items of such simplicity that meant more to me than hundreds of dollars in an envelope. A Saint Francis of Assisi book that my Grandmother signed with a simple "Richard, I love you." is priceless to me and I keep it locked in our safe. I share with my clients that this is a perfect time to give the gift of tradition and perhaps pass along a treasury of Christmas book that older family members could sign with a message for future generations to read and connect to. These items will become cherished objects and hold great sentimental value to the family. We need to look at this time of the year as an opportunity to give experiences of time well spent together and new experiences. These are gifts that will surely bring happiness and make the receiver smile when they remember the person who gifted this to them for years to come. If you do choose to give an item, make it one that you can attach a memory to and hold special meaning. If the things we give have some significance, it transforms them into cherished and memorable objects, otherwise as time goes by they will sadly become just stuff.

It was during a reading for a woman in her mid-forties that a powerful message came through from a father for his little girl. As I waited in my office for the client to arrive this older gentleman presented himself to me in my mind's eye. He was in his late seventies and had such a kind and loving presence to him. I noticed that he was tall and on the thinner side and when I noticed his hands they appeared to be well worked. Looking at his clothes, I noticed an opened button down shirt with pencils in his pocket and well-worn denim jeans. His hair was combed to the side and through his glasses I noticed his caring eyes. At times spirit comes through even before the reading begins, they are excited about the reading that's going to take place just as much as you are. When this happens, I do my absolute best to capture the information and imagery they present to me and let them know that the reading will be happening at a certain time and please join us then.

With my client sitting across from me it was time to begin, I presented the information and described the individual that was coming through. When I linked with the spirit again I began to want to talk about carpentry and working with wood. I saw before my eyes measuring, framing, notes and building with his hands. The client explained that her father was a master carpenter and could build anything. It was at this moment that her father showed me a beautiful dollhouse that he built her, I did notice that it appeared to look unfinished. The beautiful rooms and miniature furniture had so much detail and you could see the love that went into making this for his little girl. I asked her did dad not finish the dollhouse? I felt like he was telling me that his time ran out before it was done but he was happy that she still has it. He also wanted to acknowledge that it was being passed down to a younger girl, so I asked my client if she had a daughter? She replied yes I just gave the doll house to my daughter and we are doing our best to finish it together. Her eyes welled up with tears because she knew that her father was still very much present in her life and also in her family's lives. Their strong bond they had in life is still there after his death and he never left. So much more evidence was present during that reading that made her know for sure that her father was with her but the clincher was the dollhouse.

This is an example of how giving the gift of an item that someone will cherish and love could have a lasting impact on them and future generations. The love and care her father put into that small dollhouse can still be felt so many years later. Spirit always reminds us of the importance of love and that love is our connection to one another. When we put love into a gift, it's an extension of ourselves and a reminder to the receiver of the gift just how special they are to us. According to Meik Wiking (author of *The Art of Making Memories*), happy memories are essential to our mental health. They strengthen our sense of identity and purpose and bond our relationships.

Christmas Memories of Years Gone By

Memories work as powerful reminders of special moments that are dear to our hearts and help shine a light when we go through difficult times. In the midst of busy schedules, it's so important to prioritize quality time over quantity. Meaningful conversations, shared laughter, and genuine connections have a more profound impact on relationships than simply being physically present. It's so important to gather and come close during this time, share apparition and gratitude to the year that's coming to a close. We appreciate everyone that has helped us on our journey. They took the time and loved us into being and still are very much part of our lives.

My Brother Dennis and Myself During The Christmas Season

Renowned clairvoyant and known as the sleeping prophet, Edgar Cayce often spoke of the fact that we are part of a soul group, not just individuals. The souls we find in our lives are not random or accidental; rather, they are part of lives. We are not alone unless we choose to be. We belong together with others. We are both comforted by and comforting to others. Cayce's first lesson was "cooperation." Cooperation implies involvement with others. The message of Christmas is love, hope, and a new beginning. The full experience of this message is discovered when we begin anew by spreading love and hope and togetherness. Our joy is found in giving; not to be well-spoken of, or to feel personal satisfaction, but express God's love for the children, the souls in our lives.

Gordon Higginson delivered a beautiful address through trance in 1992 on Christmas Day. As he stood in front of the audience, his spirit guides brought forth this wonderful message of healing and hope. "Before you can find and discover the light, you must go into the depths of darkness. And so, your world is passing through the darkest period, when all nations are crying out for light and for peace. But the message has been taken up by the great souls and minds of those mightier ones. They have risen and sent forth messengers to come to you and gradually lead you and mankind into the great heights of the heavenly powers. These walls echo with the voices of those who once walked this Earth. Above you are the voices of those that belong to you. Surrounding you is a power that has bridged two worlds. And no longer is the bridge required, for now two worlds are one. And you have to reach for another world, a greater world, a spiritual world. A world beyond the realms of doubt and fear, where the heavenly hosts bring the power and the message of the Divine. We give you the blessings of the Spirit. May it touch the strings that lie within your heart.

Let your voice be that which comes from the being of the soul. Let your head be in the sky of the heavens. Let angel voices speak to you. Then the world will become a great light in this universe". When we read Cayce and Higginson's words we understand that we are all connected and a part of worlds within worlds. We have the ability to bridge the gap between worlds and connect with the divine. When Higginson said, "Before you can find and discover the light, you must go into the depths of darkness". For it is only when you understand the darkness you can appreciate the light.

Holiday Wellbeing

Everything in the universe is made up of energy and has its own unique vibration. The same applies to all of us incarnated on the physical plane. All of us are in a constant state of receiving and radiating energy. When we talk about positive energy it is effortless and deeply rooted in love and compassion. Dark energy is much denser and oppressive, it's rooted in fear and negativity. The holidays are a time of coming together but when we do so we need to be prepared emotionally and physically for the exchange of energy that will take place. You are only in charge of your vessel and your personal wellbeing. When you encounter negativity and the denser energy simply find a way to detach from it and seek those that resonate with you. Your energy attracts like-minded frequencies, when you're positive you attract positivity. When you have negative thoughts, you attract negativity. With feelings of anxiousness, anger or depression your frequency broadcasts your current state out into the universe and that familiar saying comes to mind "like attracts like".

We are human and experience a variety of emotions in our daily lives but it's important to know when you need to shift your way of thinking and focus on your wellbeing. If you're filling everyone's cup up but your own, it's time to focus on yourself and self-care. Bring balance into your life through exercise, relaxation, meditation and living in the moment. Know and bring awareness to your energy field, this is also known as your aura. The aura is an energy field that surrounds all living things including humans, animals and even plants. It's constantly changing from the emotions that we experience in our daily lives. This energy field encompasses the entire body and reflects the frequencies that radiate. When we feel anxiousness, negativity and anger this affects your aura. Equally if you feel fulfilled, confident and positive you will resonate in a much higher frequency and energy field. Renowned medium James Van Praagh said, "Your personal energy field contains an impression of every thought, feeling and experience you've ever had, and it's also affected by the energy fields of other people you encounter. I sometimes think we're all like giant sponges, holding onto everything that ever happened to us, and soaking up other people's energy as we encounter them".

If we're holding on to something that no longer serves us, we need to realize that it's time to let it go. James Van Praagh also said, "Forgiveness isn't excusing someone's bad behavior – it's refusing to let it harm you anymore. Holding a grudge blocks YOUR energy, so give yourself the gift of letting go". I completely agree with him and feel that we can't be a sponge and carry around other people's faults and negative baggage. Be a spiritual samurai warrior, when you are around negativity imagine cutting yourself free with a beautiful sword of white light. Any thought or worry that does not serve you for your highest good, it's time to unleash the chop-O-matic and cut yourself free. The holidays can bring with it a storm of anxiety. Knowing about energy and the light and dark, we can emotionally and spiritually be prepared for the Yuletide. Our energy is just as valuable as currency, be protective of it.

Medium Jill Marie Kelly

The holidays are usually a time of peace and love, giving and receiving, and joy. For those who have had deep losses, it can also be a very triggering time where you experience grief of the ones you've lost. Growing up, I remember my father being sad on Christmas Eve because he missed his father so much who died at the age of 59. I also had a best friend who lost his mother to brain cancer when he was in high school, so the holidays were really hard for him even though he had had young children with whom to make magic and new memories. So, I'd like to share a few things you can do to process some of your grief and create some space in your mind and in your heart for love, during the holiday season.

15 years ago, I had a reading with a client and her father came through and said, "Light a candle in my name, and I will answer to your flame." The spirit shared with me the one thing every religion got right was to light a candle for the dead. Fire can be seen in every dimension, and I have always been under the belief that everyone has psychic ability and the potential to connect to spirit. So whatever religion you are, however, you honor your loved ones, lighting a candle is a beautiful thing to do to bring their energy a little closer. When I was little and wanted to honor my grandfather, I would light a candle on Christmas Eve and write him a letter. I knew I would never send it and I knew he may never be able to receive it, but it made me feel closer to him talking about all the things in my life that I wanted him to know, all the experiences that I was having that I wished he was a part of. Deep down, I knew he was watching over me and that he was seeing everything but writing it down really helped me get some grief out of my system and feel hopeful. And sometimes even on hard days whether it was around the holidays, or if it was just an ordinary day, I would light a candle and say his name and almost feel his arms around me hugging me telling me everything would be all right. And if I didn't write a letter, I would talk about him and

tell the stories about his life to the younger generations of my family.

Richard Moschella with colleague Jill Marie Kelly

Being medium as my full time occupation, I've noticed people really want to connect to spirit around the holidays. They wish to have a conversation with their loved ones that they miss so much. One thing that is consistent every holiday season is spirit telling me to tell their loved ones to give experiences. Spirit makes it very clear that there's no luggage rack on a hearse. The memories that you make with your family and friends are what you take with you. So, spending time with dear friends or family on vacations, at concerts, at shows, in museums, driving around and looking at the holiday lights, taking the weekend trip to the shore, recharging at a bed-and-break-fast for a weekend, those types of memories that you've shared are the ones that count. So instead of giving materialistic things for the holidays, give trips, give tickets, give your time because that is the most precious thing we have.

Time is the only thing we can't get back. So, if you're feeling sad or missing your loved ones, if there are certain characteristics that you loved about the dearly departed in your family, carry on their love by creating experiences they would've loved to be a part of. Light a candle. Say a prayer. Write a letter. Give experiences. And enjoy the present moment this holiday season.

Spirit of the Holidays

Lee Grabarczyk - The Mandala Medium

Lee Grabarczyk comes from a family of intuitives and has been practicing his psychic abilities for over 40 years.

Grabarczyk, also works as an artist creating sacred geometric works of people's energies. These are designed to assist people in achieving a better understanding of themselves and inspiring a healthier self-esteem. In his role as an intuitive, he assists people in developing their intuition and a deeper understanding of the truths that lie therein. Grabarczyk says, "The identification of this authentic self allows for a more accurate starting point in one's development, serving as a checkpoint or inventory to better create a plan of action designed to positively transform one's life". He believes the principal block to our ability to identify and act on our intuition is fear. He says, "When we start to trust how real and powerful intuition is, we can improve our lives". The Process of Creating a Mandala, Dolores Canon had said that each of us has our own unique symbol and that it is found in our auric field. Grabarczyk believes he has the ability to access these symbols and render them as artwork. This physical representation has a powerful healing impact on consciousness. When Grabarczyk first meets with a client he picks up on their energy and during meditations and dream states I am given the shape that is unique to them. These drawings are then rendered as line artwork, a black and white halftone and finally in color. Shown above is an example of this process. When this book project came about I knew that I had to ask Lee to be a part of the project, he's a genuine individual in this field and takes great pride in his work. Through his artwork and readings, he brings so much healing to everyone he comes across.

This is selfless work and we are all in the service to spirit. Lee Grabarczyk is someone that truly embraces that and I'm honored to call him a friend. His insights on the spirit of the holiday and personal story remind us that love is the foundation of memories and that our loved ones are closer than you think. The following is Lee's perspective on the spirit of the holidays and this special time of year.

Lee with his Grandmother

Even in the best of times the holidays can be challenging. The planning, expectations, gift giving and seeing friends and family can be overwhelming. In spite of this most look forward to holiday get-togethers. It is a time to relive old traditions connect with the past and with some optimism looks forward to the future. A touch stone of renewal.

For some it can also be a lonely time especially with the loss of a loved one. Many remember fondly those they have lost and fervently reminisce about their memory. Over the years I have lost many. Living 66 years makes losing a loved one a likely reality. In spite of this and because of the work I do I have come to recognize the ongoing connectedness to those who are gone. When I was eight I lost my grandmother. Her connection was incredibly important to me. I felt safe in her company and her strength and love comforted me. As a child I could hardly imagine life without her.

After she died I would have dreams about her. I had them up until my early 20's. There was a rocking chair my parents had which she would sit in with me when she was alive. In my dream I would leave my room and go down a hallway and she would be there waiting for me with a big smile. In these dreams she would teach me about life and love. She shared her wisdom and this information played an important role in my maturation. I believe love is eternal. And it is the one inexhaustible resource we have. When I think of my grandmother or anyone I have lost it rekindles the energy of that connection. And yes, this can bring some sadness. More importantly it reminds me I am worthy of love because I was loved. Those I have loved who have passed are oftentimes still there with me and available to me energetically. Sometimes I will smell perfume or cigar smoke or some other scent that reminds me of someone who has passed. I feel it is their way of letting me know they are still around.

Other common symbols are birds, particularly cardinals, sometimes it is a song or even a coin like a dime that shows up seemingly randomly in my day. Each person who has passed has their own unique way of identifying themselves. About sixteen years ago my other grandmother died. At the funeral as I was crying my father said to me, "remember, we are here to celebrate her life." He was right. Every holiday when we reflect on those we have lost we can celebrate them by maintaining their traditions. This could be by preparing an entrée or dessert or snack. It may be playing a game or watching a favorite movie. I believe this is a great way of celebrating the past and the loved ones we remember. It's interesting to note how they may appear at these times.

One common example is an empty chair, a space left open even though there had been plans to have someone seated there. Others are dogs, cats or other pets fixated on a chair or a space which was commonly occupied by someone who was no longer with us. Children too are fascinating. Many will point to a spot in the air and address it by talking as if they know the spirit who is with them. Life may be short and filled with challenges but love is eternal. I prefer focusing on the latter. I think ultimately holidays give us the opportunity to reflect on those we still have in our lives. With gratitude we recognize how precious these relationships are to us and take the time to let them know how much they are loved.

The channeled messages from Maurice Borbanell of Silver Birch speak of the Christmas season and the regrowth and resurrection. Silver Birch was the spirit guide channeled by trance medium Maurice Barbanell. The teachings of Silver Birch were first published in Psychic News and Two Worlds and then as books. Silver Birch spoke about both the winter solstice season and Jesus Christ. He said that the solstice season is an important time of regrowth and resurrection, a time that the spirits receive "the greatest communion from the Great Spirit." A festival that focuses on the rebirth of the sun is important because it represents the beginning of a new cycle.

On the earth plane everything is moving forward, we spend almost all of our time living in the future. We look forward to upcoming vacations, future plans and cele-brations. Personal reflection only happens very rarely, we as a culture don't seem to have time for it anymore. I find this is also the case with individuals that are looking to develop a self-care practice, they have a hard time quieting their mind for meditation or just going within. I feel the holiday season gives us permission to linger in the past and for a little while not be too concerned with the future. We remember our past Christmas celebrations and loved ones that made the holiday so special for us. It's important to talk about those no longer physically with us, talk about them and keep their memory alive. It's an amazing way to honor them and to let future generations get to know them through your storytelling. Another great way to keep their memory alive is to start a family journal and create a place to tell your family story.

During a reading with a client that wanted to connect with her husband on the other side, she told me that she still sets a place setting at the dining room table for him at Christmas. The reading was so beautiful because he wanted to mention that she only gave him a fork. As she elaborated on the story on why he only had a fork at his place setting, I came to find out that other relatives at the table took his silverware as a joke. He came through and wanted to validate that by the end of the dinner he was only left with a fork. She walked away from that reading with an understanding that our loved ones are not gone but very much still a part of our lives and still at all our celebrations.

It's ok to set a place for them at the table, light a candle, display a photo and make something that they would have enjoyed. If you're looking for other ways to honor a deceased loved one at Christmas, consider starting a new tradition. This could be something as simple as donating to their favorite charity or planting a tree in their memory. You could also start a new family ritual, such as writing letters to your loved one or playing their favorite music. Celebrating your loved one's legacy in this manner can help you cope with the grief and honor their memory. Those on the other side of life are still connected to us, we need only to think and speak of them.

A Message of Bringing The Family Together

I can still remember one of my first mediumship readings that I had in my early twenties. I had agreed to join a friend of mine for a reading that she scheduled with a popular medium in Northern New Jersey. As we went into the mediums office, I patiently waited my turn to be read and wondered who might come through. When it was my turn, I sat down at the table and the medium explained the process of the flow of the reading. I learned to just give yes and no answers and to be open to the symbolism that would present itself. The medium closed her eyes and was quiet for a few seconds that felt like minutes. Then she opened her eyes and was looking to my side and above me, as if seeing people that were not physically in the room. She began to talk about a beloved Aunt that wanted to come through with a message and said that "the family does not gather like they use to anymore" and "it's important to get everyone together and carry on the tradition." This piece of information really hit me hard because I knew exactly what she was talking about.

I knew exactly who this Aunt was that was coming through in my reading, it was my mother's Aunt Phyllis who would always host Christmas eve parties for the family. These parties were a staple in the family and went back decades, there are even some old movie films that documented the gatherings and festivities. Watching the film flickering on the wall as the frames brought back to life those now missing physically and showing relatives from younger times. This made me think of a quote by Mitch Albom "This is a story about a family and, as there is a ghost involved, you might call it a ghost story. But every family is a ghost story. The dead sit at our tables long after they have gone". The reading came to an end and a few other loved ones in spirit came through the reading with messages. The one really powerful message was Aunt Phyllis urging the family to gather again and carry on the Christmas eve tradition. Now with so many family members not near and distance coming between them, also the melancholy of missing those no longer here physically. We needed to look beyond the sadness and grief of missing these beloved family members and understand that they are still very much present in our lives, at our celebrations and still sitting at our table. Aunt Phyllis's message was acknowledgment that she understood why we stopped coming together but it was also encouragement to gather again. If not for the older generations but for the younger ones that need the sense of family, tradition and connection to our past.

In the years since that reading our family has gathered for many Christmas eves together and enjoyed each other's company, shared stories of the past and remembered recipes for the dinner table. The family has seen another generation of children born and partake in the traditions of our family Christmas. I know without a doubt that our family members in spirit were there too, you could feel them and also hear their voices letting us know that they are ever so near.

O Christmas Tree, Give Hope and Strength Throughout the Year

During the Christmas season over 30 million trees are harvested each year. Traveling on any roadway you will see a caravan of trees tied down to the tops of cars and in the beds of trucks on their way to their temporary seasonal home. We display them in our homes and take great pride decorating them and displaying our timeless ornaments on their branches. The Christmas tree represents life and fertility and to celebrate the return of light after the dark days come to an end. The Druids believed that trees were a gift from the mother goddess, they would decorate sacred oak trees with mistletoe and lights to represent wisdom and light. Even the Romans adorned their temples with evergreens during the Saturnalia festival. The Romans considered the evergreen to be a symbol of eternal life but until the mid-19th century, Christians viewed the Christmas tree as a Pagan custom. In other places in the ancient world people hung evergreen boughs over their doors and windows, it was believed that the evergreens would keep away witches, ghosts, evil spirits and prevent illness coming into the home. Today the Christmas tree is the focal point of our yearly tradition and as we gather around it and look at the decorated branches and lights, we understand its deeper connection to our past and sacred connection to our ancestors. The Evergreens are rich with symbolic meaning during the holiday season and are at the center of ceremony and ritual.

During the start of the holiday season of 2023, my family and I headed up to a new Christmas tree farm located in Washington, New Jersey. This would be the first time in many years getting our tree at a new location, since the last farm we went to closed. As we rode through the sprawling hills and countryside of western New Jersey I could not help but take in the sites of the season. Historical churches with wreaths on their doors and home's decorated with blow up Christmas characters. Then there is the chance of seeing some vintage displays of classic Christmas blow molds that have weathered many holiday seasons and give light to the darkness of a winter's night. This year would be the second year since we lost my father in-law and it's also a time that we would all be together and trek out to the Christmas tree farm and cut down our trees. Knowing how spirit communication works and consciousness, I said quietly to myself, "Dad if you can show us a sign that you're here with us today" I also added "if you can make it a big sign." We all got out of the vehicle and jumped on the hayride that takes you through the various fields of white pines, Norway spruce, Fraser fir and blue spruce. The air was cold and fresh with the crisp and refreshing smell of pine trees. As the crowd of people descended the hayride steps and seemed to vanish in the rows of trees, it was time to select our family Christmas tree.

When we found the tree we thought would be perfect for our home, we needed to find a worker on the farm to cut it down for us. I thought to myself that this could take a while especially since so many people were probably looking for the same service. As my mother in-law went through a row of trees to get someone it seemed like only a few minutes had passed and she was walking back with a worker with a saw in hand. We greeted him and thanked him for his help and that's when I noticed his name tag on his plaid jacket. The name tag said Thomas, that was my father in-law's name. I couldn't help the tears welled up in my eyes and I thought to myself he did what he could to make that sign as big as possible. I knew he was there with us and orchestrated this incredible sign from the spirit world.

Exercise

"Raising your vibration is about feeling the love within yourself and letting your inner light shine."

I often recommend an exercise called the "meeting room," which was taught by Mavis Pittilla, who studied with the very famous medium Gordon Higginson, who started the Arthur Findlay College for mediums in England. After you get yourself to that quiet state, then imagine a meeting room, square or round, big or small. Make it any room you want, as long as it has two chairs and a picture window. Imagine yourself sitting in one of the chairs, facing the picture window, and asking for a guide or a loved one to appear. Invite them to sit with you and chat. This is an opportunity for you to hear what it's like in the spiritual dimensions from a guide, a teacher, or a loved one. You are finding out more about their world and their point of view.

You become aware of the atmosphere around you and within you, and you become aware of what the atmosphere feels like when you have another energy in it —there's a shift that you will sense. Then listen to the next thought, let them drop that in, and when you feel that energy along with that thought, you'll know the thought is from them. You begin to have these incredible insights. At times people expect a hammer over the head. It's nothing like that. It's whispers and much more subtle.

Connect with Nature

Winter is a wonderful time to connect with the natural world, as the days grow shorter the darkness and cold weather can be major deterrents to venturing into the natural world. We must not lose this connection and understand how much a vital role being in nature does for our emotional and physical health. As you begin your walk concentrate on your steps, with each step put one foot in front of the other. Once you get into the rhythm of your movement, shift your attention to your breath – inhale and exhale. Now focus on releasing what no longer serves you and breathing in the sacred prana. The life force of the natural world is a great healer and helps us shift into being present in the moment. It's about awareness and using your senses to absorb what is happening around you. The sound of birds chirping, the crush of leaves or snow under your feet, wind blowing through the branches or even the steam that is flowing along your walk. Then move onto your sense of smell and the aromas, the fresh smell of pine combined with wintery earth. The smell of leaves resting on the ground, reminds us that these leaves were once green and full of life and that a continuous circle is always at work.

Along your walk take time and just pause for a moment and look up. When we're walking, we focus on what's below us and in front of us. Take a deep breath, look up, change your perspective, notice what you see. If you don't live by a forest or natural area, you can do this by just going outside and connecting with your environment. Going within and focusing your breath and being present in the world that is happening around you. It's all about awareness and the benefits of feeling the sun on your skin and a cold breeze on your face.

Geoff Nicholson, author of *The Lost Art of Walking*, says of walking, "Your senses are sharpened. As a writer, I also use it as a form of problem-solving. I'm far more likely to find a solution by going for a walk than sitting at my desk and 'thinking.'" We must not forget about our connection to the earth and be present during this time of the year. We walk for healing, inspiration, reflection and most of all our soul.

A wonderful poet Josephine Robertson said:

> "Connecting to nature, understanding the spirituality of nature can transform our own lives. We may find our burdens lightened and our lives freer by reconnecting the shape of our lives to the natural world. We can learn to work with our inner and outer seasons instead of fighting them. And in doing so we might just learn to live with the natural world".

The forest is alive with many energies that are known as nature spirits, they bring a magical dimension to anyone who journeys off the beaten path. These etheric beings are connected to the earth, plants, flowers and other vegetation. Plant devas are rooted in mystical traditions around the world and include Hinduism and Buddhism beliefs. These beings invisible to the human eye but can be perceived through heightened states of awareness are considered plant totems and angles to the natural world. They offer guidance, protection and healing to anyone that wishes to connect. Elementals and nature spirits are connected to the four elements of Earth, Wind, Air and Water and inhabit the natural world. According to the 16th-century Swiss physician and alchemist, Paracelsus, there are four kinds of elemental:

- **Gnomes:** It's no coincidence that we have garden gnomes. Gnomes are the elementals that protect the Earth.
- **Undines:** Undines are the elementals that protect the water.
- **Sylphs:** Sylphs are the elementals that protect the air.
- **Salamanders:** Salamanders are the elementals associated with fire.

Exercise

Practice meditation or visualization:

Meditation and visualization can be powerful tools for connecting with nature spirits. Find a peaceful spot to sit quietly in nature or settle in a space where you can focus on an image or representation of a nature spirit. Visualize yourself connecting with the spirit and ask for guidance or wisdom. I also recommend journaling whatever comes into your mind during this exercise. You might be pleasantly surprised by things you write down in your journal. It's important to be present and mindful of the natural world around you and observe the plants, trees and land with curiosity and reverence.

Elemental Elves

The Yuletide is filled with stories and folklore involving elves and we can trace their origins back to Norse mythology to the *álfar*, also known as *huldufólk* 'hidden folk'. The elf character is most likely to have combined this Norse legend with other Scandinavian and Celtic cultures and myths regarding elves, fairies and nature spirits. The Elf possesses supernatural abilities and can be quite a trickster in the home during the Yule celebrations. Elves and Genomes come right of the elemental world and into our winter tales that filled our childhoods. The Christmas Elf appeared in literature around 1850 when Louisa May Alcott completed but never published a book entitled Christmas Elves. The image of the elves working in a workshop appeared in 1873 in *Godey's Lady's Book* with an illustration on the front cover of Santa surrounded by toys and elves with the caption, *"Here we have an idea of the preparations that are made to supply the young folks with toys at Christmas time"*

For centuries people have turned to the forest for meditation, solace and insight. We come into the stillness to gain a deeper state of awareness. Let's embrace the magic and unseen world that is coexisting with ours, be open to connecting with it on a deeper level. From elemental beings to seeking guidance from our guides, walking in nature is without a doubt essential for life.

CHAPTER 3

CHANNELED MESSAGES FROM THE FULCRUM

In these channeled messages from who I have gotten to know as the Fulcrum, I have gained much insight and teachings on such a deeper level. It was during a conversation with a very close friend and colleague of mine Kimberly Guyer that she asked me if I have ever tried channeling. At the time I replied that no I haven't but wanted to know more about it. We shared many conversations about how channeling works and who we are connecting with and the mechanics of it. She also told me to read and follow the work of Lee Harris, an amazing human being and soul that shares with us channeled messages from his spirit guides. Then I went on a mission to read as much as I could on the subject and then when ready to take the plunge and try it for myself.

As I sat in my office in meditation and opened up my vessel for communication, I graciously asked my guides to join me in this attempt to connect. It only took a few moments and then the messages began to flow. I asked who am I speaking with? Just like in a mediumship reading I began to hear an inner dialogue that was not coming from me but much rather coming to me. I was doing the typing as these messages were being received. They answered we are the Fulcrum, I wanted to know how many of them there were that I was communicating with. This number varies among people that channel these non-physical beings. I immediately got the number 77 and made a note of it. They are part of a collective universal consciousness and extend into galactic source energy. This means they are concerned with more than what is just happening on the earth plane. Their wisdom brings us clarity, depth and can be transformative. I felt that it would be invaluable to add it into this project and share the Fulcrums message with you, especially during the holiday season.

Just like in mediumship, when the medium connects with soul consciousness or the spirit of your loved one, they are able to get evidence based information that brings that contact back to life for the sitter. When channeling the mechanics work the same way as connecting with loved ones on the other side. I like to describe it as a radio, your antenna goes up and you raise your vibration to connect with that divine frequency. Then you tune in with your intention and wait for the contact to connect. I personally believe that we all have the ability to channel, again just like mediumship you just need to be willing to develop it and dedicate time to its unfoldment. We can all obtain guidance from our ancestors, angels, spirit guides and our higher self. I know everyone in their life has experienced inspiration and perhaps an idea or inspired vision for a new course of direction in their life or project to work on. We easily chalk it up to "I was inspired or the idea just came to me". Well, where do you think it came from? As you read these messages from who I call The Fulcrum, my team of spirit guides please keep an open mind and an open heart.

Energy and Thought

As we enter the darker months we begin to prepare and adapt just like our ancestors before us. We adjust to the short days and the longer nights and we hold those we love close to us. This is a time to take stock on oneself and go within and search your soul. What serves you and brings you happiness and fulfillment and what does not serve you. With a year coming to a close and a new year beginning, you get the opportunity to make a change and shift your perspectives. You get to choose what you want and who you want involved in your life. The life you live is manifested by your thoughts and where energy goes your thoughts flow. Be the creator of the reality you want to live and experience, dream big and dream often. Spending time in silent meditation and prayer, this is just as important as the food and water we need to consume to stay alive. We are here and always will be to offer guidance and understating from a higher perspective. We have always been and will always be. The light within and the light throughout, no one is truly alone, we are all connected by love and light. We are tethered together by this cord of immense love and light.

You must understand the power of thought and how what we think manifests in our daily life. Your thoughts can act as if there were magnets and pull into your life whatever you are contemplating and dreaming about. For those that think negatively that things will go wrong and they will never succeed, you will manifest failure. When you think about success and reaching your goals, you will succeed. Your thoughts are as valuable as currency and you need to understand that and how they will affect your life spiritually and physically. Negative minds and excuses cause stagnation and your once vibrant life becomes a barren landscape. It's like planting seeds in toxic soil that can't provide growth for the seeds and sets them up for failure. Thought is a vibration and creates a ripple effect in the collective consciousness and attracts to you what you think about.

The Christmas Spirit

When people talk about getting into the Christmas spirit we need to understand that this is a shift that they are experiencing in consciousness and one that for the most part is only temporary. Perhaps they feel inclined to donate money, time and perhaps to make decisions from a place of love rather than judgment. They often say they were in the Christmas spirit but in reality they shifted into a different thought pattern and came from a place that is heart centered. This is a place of immense love and not part of the external world. The external world makes one judge and exclude him or herself from the creator and soul consciousness. When one is in the Christmas or holiday spirit, they are coming from a place within and have shifted their perspective. This can be a permanent change only if they desire it to be. Think of how the world would be a better place if we all came from a place of love and gratitude for our fellow man. Don't just make it a shift that lasts a month, let it last a lifetime and live in soul centered bliss.

Those No Longer With Us

Being no longer with us is a misconception, they are very much still with us. The physical is no longer but the energy that made them who they were is always with us. That soul to soul connection is always with us. That never goes away or ceases to exist; it just changes and shifts. Human existence is centered around the physical but our true existence is soul to soul communication even before the physical existed. We are all souls before we are incarnated on the earth plane and always will be. We are never here or there, we need to look at this with more of a perspective of energy and quantum travel. Existing in more places than just on one plane, we are multidimensional. The human mind cannot really not comprehend but they do their best to explain it. When death occurs on the earth plane the soul is released from its vessel that it no longer desires to use or be burdened with due to weakening or limitations. There are occasions when souls leave before the body weakens and ages, these souls incarnated with exit plans that would offer those incarcerated around them lessons their souls needed to experience. The earth plane is that of a classroom and just one small stop in a multidimensional existence. Those you feel that are no longer with you are still very much present in your life and can connect with you through your internal hardware. Think in terms of energy that it cannot be created or destroyed and that the light that made your loved one who they were in life is not gone, for they have never left.

Give Yourself The Gift of Living in The Present

Humanity has a way of either living in the past or looking forward to the future. This can do your soul and life a great injustice. Being so caught up in events that you no longer can change the outcome of because they already happened or thinking of outcomes that have not happened yet, creates a void in your present life. You are neglecting the present to linger in the past or trying to peer into the future. I urge you to try to focus on the present moments in your life and your daily interactions with those that cross your path. Being present in the now is the way to live in your bliss and to bring awareness to your life. Being present will let you appreciate the moments that have been unfolding around you that you have been missing due to living in the past and future. Focusing on the now will also help you emotionally heal and can help with depression and anxiety. You create your life and project into it your thoughts and feelings; this all affects your vibration and essentially your own auric field. The auric field is an energetic field that surrounds the human body and is made up of multiple layers. These layers are connected to the body through chakras, which are the body's energy centers. Since thoughts are energy, when someone lives in the past and can't let go of negative events they can affect this sacred energy field that encompasses you.

Living in the present is a gift to all humans and lets them live in the moment and be present in all situations happening around them. You will feel more alive and bring healing to your physical and emotional wellbeing.

We Are All Connected

When we seek to touch spirit we must be ready to know our true sleeves and what is ultimately in our heart or hearts. We come to the realization that we are love and that love is the cord of all things on the mortal plane. It is the tether that keeps all connected beyond creed and ancestral connections. This is referred to in spiritualist writings as the brotherhood of man. We are all in this life at this time in space together and we are all exactly where we need to be. We once came before and most likely we will come back again. Human wants and needs interfere with your soul's divine course and progression. We lose the collective and the us and shifted more towards the I and me. We begin to see ourselves as different and not the same or equal, this is normal human thinking. This sparks wars and disharmony among people and nations. The world could be such a more beautiful and harmonic place if we realized that we are not different at all but all family connected to the divine infinite source.

We are not here to judge you but more for guidance during inner reflections and contemplation. Reaching for the inner hardware and connecting through meditation is the easiest way of tapping into our frequency. We are and have always been the light within and the light through-out. We welcome you and are always available for correspondence and guidance.

Vibration

Coming together as a collective and blending your energies all in one place is a conduit for loved ones beyond the veil to reach out. It beckons them like a lighthouse does for ships out on the ocean. Together with the common goal of sharing laughter and recalling memories this acts as a building bridge of energy to connect across the veil. There is a strength in numbers when we come together and celebrate and this allows loved ones in spirit to join in the celebration. Think of it as an exchange of energy and vibration, the music we join in and sing has its own vibration to it. The retelling of family stories has its own vibration to it. This is comparable to going to a sacred building and offering prayers and hymns to resonate and connect with the divine. In some cultures, we chant mantras that awaken our spiritual potential and bring us closer to the realization that we are all connected. So, gather and come together with the intention to honor your ancestors and join in with song and offer them glad tidings with the power of song and storytelling.

Death Is Just a Transition Into Another Form

A great metamorphosis will take place for everyone living in physical form on this planet, the inevitable is always beckoning and death looms over the horizon for you all. The finalization of it is a misconception that humans have been contemplating since the dawn of man. This is not a final destination but much rather an opportunity to free one's physical body from an earthly tether that limits the soul from soaring to its full potential. The transition into spirit is like waking up into a dream of another reality that no earthly mind could comprehend. The utter joy and love that radiates at the frequency that some call heaven or nirvana is endless and all encompassing. The metamorphosis is an ascension into the spiritual body as we say goodbye to our physical one that no longer serves us. We evolve and grow and with this embrace the greater awareness of soul to soul communication. Some humans might know this to be telepathy or simply reading one's mind. It's a sacred connection and soul language that is learned. Death is a doorway into another reality that awaits you all and the next level of knowledge on your soul's journey back home to where it began.

View

We can talk about soul perspective and how we see the bigger picture over earthly life. We have a birds eye view over all the trials and tribulations that humans will encounter during their lifetime. All the entrances and exits, the lessons that will be learned and opportunities missed. This is the greater awareness and future pull that has been and always will be. You have free will and with that the final say to choose the path that calls to you. We can only offer subtle nudges and guidance. Some might call it their conscience or a gut feeling that offers insight on an incarnated soul's path. We have and always will be here to offer guidance but ultimately you have the final decision. A way to seek the bigger picture over human decisions is to meditate on them, this allows you to establish a much stronger link with higher consciousness. This is the closest you will even in human form get a soul's perspective and that bird's eye view.

CHAPTER 4

SIGNS

As the holidays approach it's natural to think about our loved ones that are no longer here physically with us. Our memories recall the laughter and magic they brought to our celebrations during this time of year. They live on through traditions and we share stories of them to the younger generation. We do our best to recreate family recipes and to honor them at the dinner table and hope that they would be proud of our attempt to recreate memorable meals we enjoyed. It's amazing how memories can be triggered by smells and tastes and bring us to an exact moment in our life. They can also make us think of certain individuals no longer with us that are tied to these sensory memories. For some it's the smell of baking or preparing a special dish a loved one made and for others just the taste of something brings them right back to a dinner table long ago. When our loved ones in spirit choose to connect with us it's much easier for them to use our senses to pick up on their presence being around them. In some cases, people have reported smelling a mothers perfume or a fathers cologne and immediately feel their presence around them.

They reach out through signs to let us know they are still present in our daily lives and that the love they shared with us has never gone away. The relationship changed from a physical connection to a non-physical one, it's energy based and involves consciousness to connect with those on the other side of life. The spirit world is only a thought away and around everyone and everything at all times. So often we go through our daily lives with blinders on and do not notice the signs that our loved ones send us. We also discredit them by saying they are just a coincidence and nothing more than that. Life becomes overwhelming and distractions are everywhere and we need to realize that spirit is always available to provide guidance and offer us nudges to inspire and guide us.

We already have the hardware to communicate with the other side, we are all souls and are connected to the divine. It's shifting our focus and getting out of our head and allowing our soul and intuition to take over. Our soul consciousness is the source that connects to those on the other side of the veil. As we learn this new way to communicate with our loved ones in spirit we understand it's an entire new language. It involves symbolism, synchronicities and dreams, all we need to do is trust in our spirit communicators. Synchronicities remind us that there really is no such thing as coincidences and they deliver strategically orchestrated messages to offer us guidance and reassurance that we are on the right path. These synchronicities offer us a strong nudge and show us that the universe is very much a part of us all. When you learn the law of attraction, you will find that manifestation is connected to a universal frequency that allows you to actualize your dreams and make them a reality. That universal frequency that is talked about is in my opinion a huge part of soul consciousness.

Synchronicities can also be a way for our spirit guides to offer help along our path and nudge us toward a specific direction. When we notice synchronicities as a way of trying to get your attention to pause, reflect, and think deeply and sincerely about a situation we understand the power of this sacred connection. Another form of communication that the spirit world uses is symbolism. These signs appear as symbols that we encounter in our day to day lives. They can be from loved ones, spirit guides and our angels. This symbolic language offers us reassurance and guidance, it also lets us know that spirit can hear us loud and clear. Not everything you hear and see throughout your day are signs but you need to be open to receive them and interpret their meaning.

If I could suggest for you make your signs unique to the individual in spirit you're trying to establish a connection with. For example, if Dad loved his blue 1957 Chevy's, ask for that from spirit. Just be prepared that it might not come to you the way you're expecting it to. This happened to my Wife and I when we asked my Father in-law to give us a sign. He loved 57' Chevys and I said "Dad, if you're around us, we would love to see a 57' Chevy." As we drove around all day, I kept looking to see the Chevy on the road or even parked somewhere. As we went into a department store my children wandered into the toy aisle and were fixated looking at all the toy cars on the shelves. In a few moments my son Jackson emerged from the aisle holding a Hot Wheels car and asked if we could purchase it. As he turned it around I noticed its vintage look and grabbed it from his hand. He might have been a little startled as to why I grabbed it so quickly. The blue car and chrome bumper, I knew exactly what I was looking at. The bottom writing on the package read 1957 Chevy and showed me the power of establishing signs with our loved ones in spirit. If loved ones are open to it, establish signs while they are alive for afterlife communication. This makes getting the sign that was chosen between you both extremely meaningful and unquestionable when it appears in your life. It's not morbid and a conversation that should happen between you and your loved ones.

During the holiday season you may just revive a Christmas card from heaven. It might not be a physical card but a sign or symbol that brings that loved one's essence back to you. You immediately feel them near and know they are still present in your life and in your family's lives during this time of celebration. Individuals have reported having dreams during this time of year of their loved one in spirit appearing healthy and happy. A song on the radio that was their favorite or lyric captures your attention. Memories you haven't remembered in years slip into your mind, or maybe you just feel a general warm gentle presence or feel a sense of your loved ones spirit in the room. When you look at your dinner table with all the generations of family still physically with you, know that your family in spirit never left and are still sitting by your side.

Dreams

One of the most common ways the spirit world communicates with us is through dreams. It's important to pay attention to vivid or recurring dreams, as they may contain messages or symbols that hold significance for you and convey a message from a loved one on the other side.

Synchronicities

Have you ever experienced a series of meaningful coincidences? These synchronicities often serve as signs from the spirit world. Pay attention to *repetitive numbers, unexpected encounters*, or situations that seem too perfect to be mere chance.

Electronic Disturbances

Spirits can manipulate electronic devices as a way to get our attention. Pay attention to unexplained malfunctions with your phone, computer, or other electronic devices. It could signify that the spirit world is trying to communicate with you.

Mother & Daughter Christmas Dinner

It was after a mediumship gallery reading that an attendee came up to the stage and wanted to tell me a story that involved her mother that was in spirit. As the reading was going on I wanted to keep talking about her mother and a very strong floral perfume that she wore. I knew without a doubt that her daughter has felt her around, her mother very lovely wanted her presence to be known. When I asked if she felt and especially smelled a perfume mom wore, her eyes filled up with tears. I told her that her mom is extremely strong willed and she wants to acknowledge the help that she provided to her, especially at the end of her life. More evidence was accepted and I moved on to other attendees and concluded the event. When the gallery reading ends I always stay behind to talk and thank all the attendees for coming. This is a special time for me because some that received readings elaborate on the messages that came through. The woman with the mom, who wore the strong perfume wanted to share where exactly she smelled the perfume. She went on to tell me that she was at the grocery store doing her holiday shopping.

This would be a trip that they took together as they would prepare the menu for Christmas dinner. This was the first year that she had to do the shopping on her own and she found it extremely difficult. She found herself at times just staying down the long aisles and thinking about her mother. When she managed to get everything to the checkout line that's when the familiar floral perfume smell came out of nowhere. She asked the cashier and shopper in front of her if they smelled the perfume, they both said no. The woman said the smell only lasted a minute and then went away, she checked out and sat in her car and began to cry. She knew without a doubt that her mom continued their holiday shopping trip together and was with her that day. This is the power and intelligence of the spirit world, and how they show up in our lives every day.

Smoke and Forgiveness

Another woman shared with me her experiences of smelling smoke, wherever she went. She described it as if someone was smoking close by and she could not see who it was. This went on for months and she asked me what I thought it meant. I immediately connected with her father and he presented himself to me with so much regret in life towards his children and his behavior. He also was coming close to her now since the passing of her husband to connect with his child and ultimately seek forgiveness and let her know that he is close. When I conveyed what was coming through with my mediumship, she immediately shut down the communication and explained how they did not get along and how she disliked her father very much. She also added since his passing many years ago, she did not even visit his gravesite. The woman wanted the smoke and message to be some else entirely and not her deceased father. This woman was one of three sisters and the other two sisters said without a doubt they had been smelling smoke too and it smelled like the cigarettes that their father had smoked for years. They had a different relationship with their father and were open to communication and knowing that he was trying to make his presence known. I ended the session with the woman and we talked briefly about forgiveness and what that does for the living and the so-called dead. Forgiving other people doesn't mean that you excuse their actions and does not require you to become vulnerable again. Forgiveness is something you do for yourself and for your emotional and physical well-being. This causes an energetic ripple I feel in the spirit world and can be felt through soul consciousness and provides healing for the living and the dead. We are all connected at a soul level, holding onto negative feelings about another person causes negative vibrations in ourselves. Once we cross over into the spirit world, our earthly life and choices we made become clear to us and a great lesson takes place.

We soulfully grow and evolve and realize what we did and didn't get right. Most call this process our life review and this happens at physical death.

This woman was not ready to accept the contact of her father and it's completely fine, as a medium I'm only acting as the telephone for the spirit world. Through what I conveyed I hope I planted the seed of forgiveness and one day she can find the peace she needs to heal her life and this relationship on the other side.

Moschella Mediumship Gallery Reading

<u>Cardinals: Messengers of The Spirit World</u>

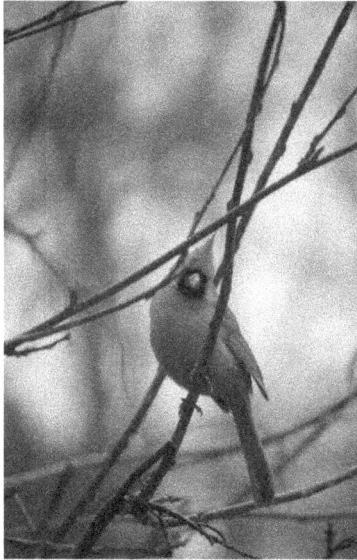

For many the Cardinal is a bird that symbolizes a visit from a loved one from heaven. This belief can be traced back to the Native Americans, they believed that the cardinal was sent to us by our ancestors and the bird brought a message of hope, kindness and a deeper connection to past ancestors. Over time and through different cultures the cardinal took on a symbolic meaning. Many began to associate them with messages from heaven or from a departed loved one. These heavenly visitors have brought assurance to many going through the grief of losing a loved one. They offer encouragement and at times stop us in our tracks and bring a loved one's memory near just by seeing the beautiful red bird. In the bleakness of winter, the beauty of the cardinal can bring color into our lives and offer hope during tough times.

I have gotten many signs from cardinals over the years but in all of my readings I make sure I tell the audience to look for the symbolism in other places as well. A visit from the bird is extremely special but some may argue that they are a very common bird in the winter. So, to make them showing up in your life extremely special and to take coincidence off the table. Remember that it symbolizes a deeper meaning and we do not necessarily have to see the physical bird at our doorstep to know we're receiving a sign from the other side. I have been driving on highways, when an eighteen wheeler speeds past me with Cardinal Trucking on the side of it. I have gotten cardinal through packages that were delivered with a cartoon of a cardinal on the box, talk about the cardinal being on your doorstep. I have seen cardinals show up in decals on vehicles to be on a real estate billboard as I drove through a town heading to an event. The thing to remember is to always be open to symbolism and look at it in other areas of our lives. Sometimes it happens in very subtle ways but when you realize how to establish signs with our loved ones, you get a sense of how incredible our connection with them is.

Signs can be whatever you want them to be, I always say make it something meaningful to the both of you. So, when the sign shows up in your life it's meaningful and connects you to your loved one. Don't pick something that is too common and spirit loves a good challenge, so think outside the box. This also makes receiving the sign incredibly impactful when you get it. It could be a loved one's song that plays on the radio after asking them to let you know they are around. We just need to be open enough to notice it and realize that they can in fact hear us. One of the greatest books that I recommend on signs is by medium and author Laura Lynne Jackson. Jackson says,

> "Our loved ones on the Other Side send us signs designed to make us think of them. They do so to remind us that they are still connected to us in very real and powerful ways. The love that bound us here on earth continues to connect us after they've crossed. The interests we shared, the joys we had in common, the memories that make us laugh—these are all part of the ongoing and everlasting connection between us and the Other Side."

CHAPTER 5

SPIRITS MESSAGE
PRAYER, FORGIVENESS, REGRETS AND LIVING LIFE

As a spiritual being that appreciates our ancient connection to the Yuletide and Christmas season, I can't help but to see the mixing of traditions both old and new. The darkness and the light are intertwined with pagan and Christian beliefs that bring richness and traditions to this winter celebration. We gather and partake in traditions that have been passed down from generations before us. These rituals create a sense of belonging and togetherness and ultimately impact our mental health. They fulfill the "Four B's" Being, Belonging, Believing and Benevolence. They give our lives meaning and the sense of connection with each other. Traditions can ground us in our ever changing lives and help create memories that will last a lifetime. What we also do by carrying on these traditions that our loved ones, now on the other side of the veil did with us is connect with them. Just the thought of, "This is what I did with my grandmother or my dad's recipe" connects with what I like to call their soul consciousness. It works just like a prayer and can be felt by all in the spirit world.

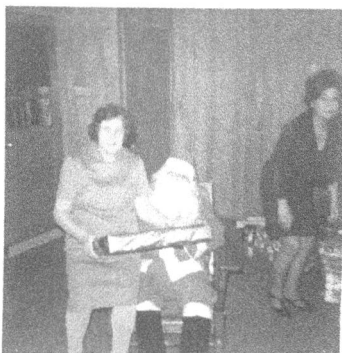

My Great Grandmother Martha with Santa Claus

<u>Prayer</u>

Gordon Higginson spiritualist medium and teacher said "Surely it is our loved ones, those who are closest to us who will hear us and those who have been given spiritual charge of our welfare upon earth. Prayer is not all about asking, demanding even, when we think that we are asking for the right things. Prayer is listening, communicating, being at one with reality and the reality of God. In prayer, we become our God. And if we listen, we are given the answers, the strength and knowledge to see through our troubles not from an outside source, but from our inner reality". This is the most selfless and heart centered place to come from, to connect with your past ancestors and carry on their beliefs and values. In doing so, we honor them and they know it.

Forgiveness

The spirit world is around everyone and everything, our loved ones are not in some far away place that is unattainable. We can reach out and connect on a soul level and bridge the veil between two worlds for soul to soul contact. As a medium and spiritual teacher, seeing someone's face light up when I communicate with a loved one on the other side or teach them about our connection to the spirit world, brings me fulfillment and joy. It's a privilege to work with spirit and to serve as the instrument for them to use for communication. Through many readings I have delivered many messages from our spirit communicators about forgiveness and regrets they had in life. This is a great teaching moment because this shows us, while we are incarnated on the earth plane to bring forgiveness to people and situations that have had impacted our lives. These words from John O'Donohue are extremely powerful, "forgiveness is one of the really difficult things in life, the logic of receiving hurt seems to run in the direction of never forgetting, either the hurt or the hurter, when you forgive some deeper divine generosity takes over you, when you can forgive then you are free". Forgiveness is echoed in A Christmas Carol, Scrooge learns to forgive and see the error of his ways. He then sees the virtue and goodness of forgiveness and changes his life for the better.

<u>Regrets</u>

As we go through our lives we can get caught up in our day to day tasks and appointments. We find ourselves at times on a daily autopilot to complete our work and completing our adult duties. It's incredibly easy to lose focus on yourself and your personal dreams. Life moves by incredibly fast and before you know it, another decade has passed. When communicating with the other side and I bring forth messages from spirit, they talk about regrets and things they wish they realized in life. Even individuals on their deathbed have said, "I wish I'd had the courage to live a life true to myself, not the life others expected of me". When people realize that their life is almost over and look back clearly on it, it is easy to see how many dreams have gone unfulfilled. Most people had not honored even a half of their dreams and had to die knowing that it was due to choices they had made, or not made.

In one reading a woman's husband came through and showed me a beautiful sailboat and going out on the water. He also showed me watching beautiful sunsets and enjoying a glass of wine. I was being drawn up into New York State and knew the area was Lake George. I mentioned all this to my sitter and she confirmed that her husband always talked about vacationing at Lake George. She went on to tell me that he would always talk about buying a sailboat and getting away to the Lake George area. They shared this dream together for many years, but the only thing that got in the way of making this dream a reality was his work schedule. He was an amazing husband, she said, but he would always be working. We got into plenty of arguments over this during our marriage. He always said he needed to work hard for our future and for retirement. The only thing we did not know was that our eleven year marriage would come to an end in the summer of 2015, he was diagnosed with advanced cancer and we needed to prepare for the end. As he laid in the hospital bed we would talk about many what if's and the sailboat would always come up and go to Lake George.

Getting this information about the evidence her husband presented was so important because he wanted to express to her his regrets about losing himself in his work and putting his dream on hold for tomorrow. This is also a story that gives us all a nudge to live in the present, the future is not promised to anyone. It is very important to honor at least some of your dreams along your life's path. Be open to new opportunities and try to create space in your life to cultivate your dreams into reality. Many people suppress their feelings in order to keep peace with others. As a result, they settled for a mediocre existence and never became who they were truly capable of becoming. As long as you choose kindness over being right and your words are not used to wound someone else, say what you need to say now. In the end the only thing we get to take with us is the Love and Knowledge that we obtained in this lifetime on earth. It all comes down to the love that we shared and that we lived fully and enjoyed every minute of our lives.

Moschella During A Gallery Mediumship Reading

A medium can connect with our loved ones on the other side and help bring healing to someone's pain. When these connections happen the result is life changing when the sitter becomes aware of the continuity of life and that the light that made their loved one who they were in life did not die with the physical body, but still exists and is ever so close. Perhaps they leave the reading with just a little less grief than what they can into the reading with, then I feel that I served spirit well in the reading. A mentor of mine through her teachings and book, Coral Polge said we are only telephone lines for spirit to communicate through. Our spirit communicators deserve all the credit and we are only the vessels. Spirit really deserves the credit for working through us and showing us that we are so much more than just our physical bodies. They also teach us that we need to live and also forgive and not put off till tomorrow what can be done today. The importance of connecting to the divine through prayer and communicating with those on the other side of the veil. Also, the courage to live a life that is true to yourself and give love every chance you get. In a way it's like embracing and living in the Christmas spirit throughout the year but mostly it's about living a well lived life.

The Power of Song

"Music is the mediator between the spiritual
and the sensual life."
- Ludwig van Beethoven

The Spirit would also inspire us, many artistic individuals that say they woke up with a melody in their head, song lyrics, painting or even the idea of a book. This inspiration comes in all forms and happens to everyone. I truly feel that this is spirits way of nudging us along our path and helping us manifest something that will benefit humankind. Inspiration comes in all forms, when we are inspired. Wayne Dyer said, "When you are inspired by a great purpose, everything will begin to work for you." Dyer also throughout his work quoted Patanjali, "When you are inspired by some great purpose, some extraordinary project, all of your thoughts break their bonds. Your mind transcends limitations; your consciousness expands in every direction; and you find yourself in a new, great and wonderful world. Dormant forces, faculties and talents become alive and you discover yourself to be a greater person than you ever dreamed yourself to be." The story I heard about "The Bells On Christmas Day" really resonated with me and is a beautiful inspired work. Longfellow, who experienced so much tragedy and could have easily given up on hope and faith, penned a song that will last forever.

Henry Wadsworth Longfellow

Henry Wadsworth Longfellow had fallen into a depression in 1861 when his second wife Frances died. She had been sealing envelopes with hot wax when a flame caught her clothes on fire. Henry had rushed to her aid and tried to smother the flames. But by the time the fire was out, Frances had been burned beyond recovery. She died the next day. Henry, burned badly as well, was too sick to attend her funeral. The death marked a turning point in Longfellow's life. His physical appearance changed dramatically as he began growing his beard because the burns disfigured his face. Mentally, he sank into depression. Their Eighteen year marriage was the happiest time of his life. In the wake of her death, he spent much of his time translating other works and less on his own writings. On Christmas day in 1862 he would record in his journal:

"A merry Christmas' say the children, but that is no more for me."

And even 18 years later he would still be mourning Frances' loss, when he wrote:

The Cross of Snow

In the long, sleepless watches of the night,

A gentle face—the face of one long dead—

Looks at me from the wall, where round its head

The night-lamp casts a halo of pale light.

Here in this room she died; and soul more white

Never through martyrdom of fire was led

To its repose; nor can in books be read

The legend of a life more benedight.

There is a mountain in the distant West

That, sun-defying, in its deep ravines

Displays a cross of snow upon its side.

Such is the cross I wear upon my breast

These eighteen years, through all the changing scenes

And seasons, changeless since the day she died.

In 1863, Longfellow's son, Charley enlisted in the American Civil War and joined the 1st Massachusetts Artillery, against his father's wishes. Longfellow feared for his son's future. In June, Charley came down with a fever. Longfellow went to Washington and brought him back to spend summer on leave at the family cottage in Nahant, Mass. Though committed to the fight, the romance of war was stripped away for Charley in the coming months of battles. In one letter home, he described seeing a fellow soldier lose his leg and other close calls "They may talk about the gaiety of a soldier's life but it strikes me as pretty earnest work when shells are ripping and tearing your men to pieces." In November, Charley's own luck ran out. At New Hope, Virginia his unit was engaged in a battle and he was shot. The bullet went through his back to shoulder, just nicking his spine. Again, Longfellow had to travel to Washington to retrieve his son from the hospital. They arrived back at their Cambridge home on

December 8, and a grim Longfellow set about the months-long process of trying to nurse his son back to health. On Christmas day, 1863, Longfellow a 57-year-old widowed father of six children, the oldest of which had been nearly paralyzed as his country fought a war against itself, wrote a poem seeking to capture the dynamic and conflict in his own heart and the world he observes around him. He found in them a message that peace would come again to the troubled nation. They inspired him to write the poem, Christmas Bells.

I heard the bells on Christmas Day

Their old, familiar carols play,

And wild and sweet

The words repeat

Of peace on earth, good-will to men!

And thought how, as the day had come,

The belfries of all Christendom

Had rolled along

The unbroken song

Of peace on earth, good-will to men!

Till, ringing, singing on its way,

The world revolved from night to day,

A voice, a chime,

A chant sublime

Of peace on earth, good-will to men!

Then from each black, accursed mouth

The cannon thundered in the South,

And with the sound

The carols drowned

Of peace on earth, good-will to men!

It was as if an earthquake rent

The hearth-stones of a continent,

And made forlorn

The households born

Of peace on earth, good-will to men!

And in despair I bowed my head;

"There is no peace on earth," I said:

"For hate is strong,

And mocks the song

Of peace on earth, good-will to men!"

Then pealed the bells more loud and deep:

"God is not dead; nor doth he sleep!

The Wrong shall fail

The Right prevail,

With peace on earth, good-will to men!"

Charley never did return to fight, despite his wish to. He was honorably discharged in February of 1864. Longfellow's poem, published originally in a magazine, would be set to music in 1872, but with the middle stanzas often removed. The song has been covered by many artists and still plays throughout homes over the Christmas season. As I get older I appetite this song and its message so much more. It reminds us that God is ever present in our lives, conflicts will end as long as one has faith anything is possible.

Count Your Blessings (Instead of Sheep)

This popular song written by Irving Berlin was used in the classic 1954 film White Christmas and cemented it as a Christmas classic. Even though the song does not reference the Christmas season it has been part of the holiday season since it appeared in the classic film. The song came about from a personal experience that Berlin was having, he was having terrible insomnia brought on by stress. In a letter to 20th Century Fox executive Joseph Schenck, Berlin wrote, "I'm enclosing a lyric of a song I finished here and which I am going to publish immediately...You have always said that I commercialize my emotions and many times you were wrong, but this particular song is based on what really happened. The story is in its verse, which I don't think I'll publish. As I say in the lyrics, sometime ago, after the worst kind of a sleepless night, my doctor came to see me and after a lot of self-pity, belly-aching and complaining about my insomnia, he looked at me and said, "speaking of doing something about your insomnia, did you ever try counting your blessings?"

The song reminds all of us that we have been absolutely blessed throughout our lives and we should not worry and let short term problems trouble us. There is inspiration that is involved, when composing a musical piece or having lyrics come out of either to heal and inspire. Whether you believe that it's coming from the higher self, spirit guides or a divine source. Many musicians all share experiences of getting melodies and lyrics in their sleep states and waking up and composing what came to them or the lyrics of a song. I feel music is very intuitive and the spirit world is always inspiring and doing what they can to heal and offer guidance through music.

These songs become timeless and are essential to our holiday rituals and celebrating the season. They have a deep connection to our faith and lives while we are incarnated on the earth plane. In terms of vibration, music can heal and has been at the center of the human experience. As we celebrate the Yuletide and gather for Christmas, we come together and raise our voices and sing songs that are ageless. This too is part of the ritual of honoring the season that has been part of the fabric of the holiday season. Our voices and the music join a collective and offer a vibration of hope and glad tidings for the season and new year to come.

<u>Playlist for Your Celebrations</u>

- I Heard the Bells on Christmas Day - Frank Sinatra
- Count Your Blessings (Instead of Sheep) - Rosemary Clooney
- Song for a Winter's Night - Gordon Lightfoot
- Silent Night - Various artists
- It Came Upon The Midnight Clear - Various
- Christmas Must Be Tonight - The Band
- A Dreamer's Holiday - Willie Nelson
- Pretty Paper - Roy Orbison
- I Saw Three Ships - Sting
- The Spirit of Christmas - Joe Sabolick
- Everyday Will Be Like A Holiday - Eric Clapton
- The Holly And The Ivy - Various
- O Tannenbaum - Various
- Deck The Halls - Various
- Here We Come a Wassailing - Various

CHAPTER 6
YULETIDE SYMBOLISM AND RITUAL

As we gather and celebrate with our family and friends, look around the table and absorb all the individuals you're celebrating the holiday with. Be present in the moment and know the ancient traditions of the Yuletide are all around you. Celebrate together, recall memories and share in the cheer and laughter. Your ancestors would not want this to be a time of grieving but rather a time to celebrate life and a new year to come. When you look around at the decorations and symbolism you will have a greater sense of the ancient connection to the Yuletide and how we have incorporated it into our homes during the holiday season.

Just like the Yule tree, one of the most prominent symbols for early Pagans. The tree represented life itself and was adorned with pinecones, berries, fruit, corn and coins. This was done in hopes of attracting abundance and prosperity in the new year. In the 1840's Queen Victoria took a trip to Germany and fell in love with the Yule tree and wanted to have one. This is how the tradition of the Christmas tree was born. So much symbolism of the modern holiday we take for granted has deeper meaning and connection to the Yuletide. The traditions of old and new come together and are interwoven into our families celebrations.

Evergreens for Yule: Symbols of Renewal

Evergreens were cut and brought indoors to symbolize life, rebirth and renewal. They were thought to have power over death because their green never faded, and they were used to defeat winter demons and hold back death and destruction. Because of their strength and tenacity, they were also believed to encourage the Sun's return.

Holly: Yule Symbol of Hope

Holly, which represents the masculine element, was often used to decorate doors, windows and fireplaces. Because of its prickliness it was thought to capture or ward off evil spirits before they could enter a home and cause harm. The holly leaves, symbolic of the Holly King, represent hope, while the red berries represent potency.

Mistletoe: Yule Traditions

Mistletoe, which represents the female element, also holds much importance as it was used by Druid priests in special ceremonies during the Winter Solstice. They believed that its green leaves represented the fertility of the Mother Goddess, and its white berries, the seed of the Forest God or Oak King. Druids would harvest the mistletoe from sacred oak trees with golden scythes and maidens would gather underneath the trees to catch the falling branches, preventing them from falling to the ground; for if this happened, it was believed that all sacred energy in the plant would pour back into the earth. The branches and sprigs were then divided and distributed to be hung over doorways as protection against thunder, lightning and other evils. Mistletoe was also worn as an amulet for fertility or hung above the headboard.

Yule Tree: An Important Pagan Symbol

The Yule Tree was also another important symbol in pagan tradition. Originally, it represented the Tree of Life or the World Tree among early pagans. In ancient times it was decorated with gifts people wanted to receive from the gods. It was adorned with natural ornaments such as pinecones, berries and other fruit, as well as symbols sacred to the gods and goddess. In some holiday traditions, garlands of popcorn and berries were strung around the tree so that visiting birds could feed off the tree as well.

The Yule Log

The custom of burning the Yule Log began with the ancient Scandinavians who burned a huge log, felled from an Ash tree, to honor their god Thor. In the Celtic tradition, a continual hearth fire was kept preventing spirits from entering the home. In order for the fire to keep burning, a large Oak tree was felled and brought into the home where the tree was placed trunk first into the hearth, with the last remnants set aside to burn with next year's fire. It was also believed that the longer the Yule log burned, the faster the sun would come to warm the earth.

Candles

Another way to have an eternal flame within the home. They symbolized the light and warmth of the sun and were used to chase away evils and lure back the returning sun/son. They also are a great way to offer remembrance to our ancestors on the other side of the veil and are deeply connected with many religions.

Wreaths

Were also traditional in ancient times for they symbolized the wheel of the year and the completion of another cycle.

They were made of evergreens and adorned with cones and berries and hung as decoration throughout the home. They were also given as gifts to symbolize the infinity of goodwill, friendship and joyfulness.

Bells

Bells are often rung during the Winter Solstice to drive away demons that surfaced during the dark time of the year. They were rung in the morning as everyone began to wake to chase away the dark days and herald in the warmer, brighter days following the solstice.

Elves

Elves first became associated with Yule because the ancients knew that the Spirits that created the Sun inhabited the land of Elves. By including elves in the Yule celebrations, the ancients believed they were assuring the elves assistance in persuading the Sun to return. They have powerful energy and are enchanting, they are slightly different then the Fae or Faery folk. Elves call out to all those that have a connection to this realm, they offer balance and apparition for the land and forests. They bring balance and also merrymaking to all those that seek them. The Elves are keepers of ancient secret magical knowledge which they are willing to impart to those who are ready to assist with their work. They work alongside the Fairies and Gnomes.

Gingerbread

Gingerbread was considered to be a specialty bread during this time since ginger had not been available until the Crusaders brought it back in the 11th century. There were strict laws regarding specialty breads in that time, so gingerbread was only allowed to be produced during the holidays and thus, it became associated with winter and Yule.

Wassail

Derives from the Old English words *waes hael*, which means "be well", "be hale" or "good health". It is a strong drink, usually a mixture of ale, honey and spices for mulled apple cider. When pagans went into the forest to fell the great oak for the Yule log, they would anoint the tree with wassail and bedeck them with wassail-soaked cakes, thus the ritual of wassailing was born. At home, the wassail would be poured into a large bowl during feast time and the host, when greeting his or her guests, would lift a drink and wish them "waes hael", to which they would reply "drinc hael", which meant "drink and be well".

Caroling

Caroling was also a popular Yule tradition when young children honored the Winter Solstice with song. They would go through the villages, singing door to door. The villagers, in return, would reward them with tokens and sweets and small gifts which symbolized the food and prosperity given by the Mother Goddess to all her Earthly children. Also, the act of singing raises our spirits and sends out vibration into the universe. Songs of love and tradition are all part of the Yuletide ritual. This connects us to our past and also the sea of soul consciousness and permeates all realms. In religions we sing, pray and recite mantras to offer remembrance and to connect to the divine.

Storytelling

One of the best ways to incorporate the spirit of Yule into the lives of children is through stories encompassing the tone of the holiday. If you're looking for Scandinavian folklore I highly suggest The Tomten by Astrid Lundgren. If you're looking for something encompassing the Old Norse lore of Yuletide, Old Mother Frost will provide your family with the magical and cozy messages everyone wants for the season. Storytelling is a captivating way to convey, honor and share the magic of traditions with young children and adults.

Yule wreath

Make a wreath of evergreens (like yew, holly, pine, mistletoe, and ivy) to represent everlasting life, protection, and prosperity. Besides being seasonal, the yew tree is traditionally associated with eternity and reincarnation, holly and ivy ward off negative energy, pine has healing magic, and mistletoe brings fertility and abundance.

- Evergreen plants like pine, mistletoe, fir, juniper, holly, and cedar. You can use branches, pinecones, and berries.
- Candles, particularly ones in Yule colors of red, green, or gold.
- Crystals in the same colors, such as emerald, ruby, and carnelian.
- Symbols of winter, such as snowflake decor or even a small bowl of melted snow.
- Symbols of the Sun, such as a Sun charm or the Sun tarot card.
- Bells—traditionally used to drive away evil spirits and to promote harmony
- Winter produce, such as chestnuts, apples, and oranges.

The Oak King & Holly King

Illustration of the Oak King and Holly King

Oak King and Holly King represented personifications of summer and winter. They were locked in a never-ending battle for seasonal supremacy. Both Kings represented solar lightness, darkness, crop renewal, and growth. During the warm days of summer and when in full leaf, the Oak King is at the height of his strength. On the approach of winter and with the loss of the Oak King's leaves, the Holly King regains power which peaks at the winter solstice. At this point the Oak King is reborn. As his new leaves open, the cycle perpetuates. Both are portrayed in familiar ways with the Holly King as a woodsy version of Father Christmas dressed in red with sprigs of holly in his hair. The Oak King is portrayed as a fertility god-like figure appearing as a green man or similar forest charac-ter. The story of the Oak King and Holly King symbolize the changing of the seasons and the continuous circle of life and death.

Imagery and Yuletide Symbolism -Lafayette, New Jersey

Light a Yule Log

Yule log burning is a symbolic ritual to release the past and banish old or negative energy that you don't want to follow you into the new year. It's also a way to welcome back the Sun and celebrate the fact that the days are going to get lighter from now on.

Do a Yule Ritual

Think about your resolutions and intentions for the coming year. Light a candle and speak your resolutions out loud, then sit with the candle and let it burn down as you visualize your ambitions coming true. Imagine the positive rewards, daydream about living this new lifestyle, and then write down actionable steps for making your daydream a reality.

Declutter Your Space

Yule is a release of the old to get ready for the new, so it's the perfect time to do some yuletide cleaning. When you've completed the physical cleaning process, spiritually cleanse your home—I like smoke cleansing by burning plants like pine needles and mistletoe.

CHAPTER 7
FAMILY RECIPES & THE SPIRIT OF SAINT NICHOLAS

We must remember the importance of tradition when it comes to preparing our holiday menus. This is the time to honor family recipes that have been passed down from one generation to another. It's through our sense of taste that we are transported back to Christmases long ago, if we closed our eyes only for a few seconds time travel seems possible. The smell of Christmas cookies brings me back to the Christmas eve table, and my childhood. My great aunts would have these beautiful cookies in the shape of Christmas trees on a large dish in the middle of the desert table. The green, yellow, red and chocolate frosting beckoned me to keep sampling these tasty treats. It was through cooking and baking that a family showed its love and caring for those gathered at the table. The preparation and consumption of food is linked to the holiday and to everyone's memories. Through medi- umship readings Spirit always shares a connection to preparing food for their loved ones and the sharing of recipes.

Grandma Sestanovich in Her Element

Spirit even at times acknowledges that a loved one is using their recipe and is doing a great job but playfully says "mine was better". This is always a touching and funny moment when spirit comes through with an acknowledgement and critique of the current cook. Through our family recipes we remember, taste and feel the love that surrounds us. I want to share a few recipes that have been in my family for generations with you and pass along these beautiful and tasty memories.

Clairgustance is a unique psychic ability that lets people taste substances without them touching their tongue. It's part of a broader category of psychic phenomena where information is received beyond the traditional five senses. Clairgustance can happen during readings to the medium and help them explain a certain taste they start to receive from spirit. This can also help the reading and provide evidence based information to the sitter. As the medium begins to describe the taste that's connected to the spirit that's coming through in the reading the sitter can confirm or deny the information. Clairgustance demonstrates the interplay between our senses and the brain. This is where memory, emotion come together and create intuitive taste responses during the reading.

You don't need to be intuitive or a medium to immediately be transported by the smell or taste of food. This is how powerful these memories are and the spirit world knows that. This is why when spirit comes close they use these senses to communicate their presence to us. In so many cases experiencers describe smelling things that remind them of their loved one. Some tell stories of almost tasting moms pasta sauce or baking and that brings them comfort. Spirit always amazes me at how they communicate with us and show up in our daily lives.

During a gallery reading with Lisa Morrison in Hudson's Mill in Gardnerville, New York I began to get the taste of anisette in my mouth. As this was happening I began to see in my mind's eye, an older gentleman and he was showing me a tray of cookies. Then for some reason I saw the image of Sesame Street's Cookie Monster. Now this reading was getting wild and I could not help but ask "was the man a cookie monster and did he like anisette cookies?". The sitter receiving the reading exclaimed that he loved anisette cookies and they all teased him by calling him a cookie monster. This is what I mean by spirit, always amazing me by how they come through with information during readings. The importance of food is one of the cornerstones in many readings, when spirit provides evidence for the living and it ties into traditions.

Owen Moschella Keeping A Close Eye on the Christmas Cookies

The Spirit of Saint Nicholas

It was during the winter of 2020 that my next door neighbors Cindy and John were preparing to move. I was getting out of my car in the driveway, when John called over to me with a question. He was holding a black garbage bag in his hand and asked if I was interested in a Santa Claus costume. I thought about it for a few seconds and told him I would definitely take it. My wife and I welcomed our first son Jackson a year earlier and it would be good to have for the future, since the real Santa is extremely busy. I thought It would be a great way to help the big man out and spread some Christmas cheer. A few weeks later the cancer hospital that I work at asked if anyone would want to play Santa Claus for their patients. I couldn't help but see the synchronicity in all of this and how I just got the costume a few weeks earlier. Doing what I do, I know a nudge from spirit when it happens and this definitely was a big nudge.

So, I agreed to be Santa Claus for the cancer hospital and choose a few dates for the arrival of the jolly old elf. In the weeks leading up to Santa's arrival I wanted to know more about Saint Nicholas. I read everything I could get my hands on and found out that he was born during the third century in the village of Patara in Asia Minor. Today it would be Southern Turkey and he had wealthy parents that raised him to be a devout Christian. His parents became ill and died in an epidemic when Nicholas was very young. With his inheritance Nicholas helped the sick, suffering and gave money to the poor. He deactivated his life to being in the service of God and was made Bishop of Myra. Bishop Nicholas became known throughout the land for his generosity to those in need, his love for children, and his concern for sailors and ships.

My Best Santa Impersonation

Under the Roman Emperor Diocletian, who ruthlessly persecuted Christians, Bishop Nicholas suffered for his faith, was exiled and imprisoned. The prisons were so full of bishops, priests, and deacons, there was no room for the real criminals, murderers, thieves and robbers. After his release, Nicholas attended the Council of Nicaea in AD 325. He died December 6, AD 343 in Myra and was buried in his cathedral church. Through the centuries and generations many stories and legends have been told of St. Nicholas' life and deeds. These accounts help us understand his extraordinary character and why he is so beloved and revered as protector and helper of those in need.

There are many legends of his deeds but this one truly encapsulates the selfless and giving nature of Saint

Nicholas. There was a poor man with three daughters. The family was so poor, there was no money for the girls' dowries. They would remain unmarried and be forced into prostitution to support themselves. And even if they didn't take up the profession, everyone would think they had. Nicholas wanted to help them anonymously, so he went to the house by night. Every night the girls hung their stockings by the fire to dry. Nicholas threw a bag of gold through the window. It landed in the eldest girl's sock. The same thing happened the next two nights. Imagine the surprise and joy experienced in the humble house. The girls could marry after all and live a normal life.

The name Santa Claus evolved from Nick's Dutch nickname, Sinter Klaas, a shortened form of Sint Nikolaas (Dutch for Saint Nicholas). In 1804, John Pintard, a member of the New York Historical Society, distributed woodcuts of St. Nicholas at the society's annual meeting. The background of the engraving contains now-familiar Santa images including stockings filled with toys and fruit hung over a fireplace.

In 1809, Washington Irving helped to popularize the Sinter Klaas stories when he referred to St. Nicholas as the patron saint of New York in his book, *The History of New York*.

With my deep dive into the history of Saint Nicholas and his connection to Santa Claus, I was ready to transform and put on the red suit and make my big appearance.

When the day arrived at the cancer hospital, I put the suit and make up on and made my way out to the lobby. I would be standing next to a Christmas tree and greeting patients when they came in and out of the building. The suit was extremely hot and my mind drifted to the work that I was missing and how I was going to probably be behind in my work when this Santa appearance was over. Patients walked over to me and took photos and exchanged small talk with Santa. Some asked if they were good this year and if they would be receiving presents and others simply said thank you.

Then there was one patient who walked up and put their arms around me and gave me a big hug and asked for a photo. Their voice trembled a little and when our eyes met I could see the eyes looking back at me welling up with tears. The kind older man leaned into my ear and said "you're my last Santa Claus" we embraced for a few moments and then he made his way through the lobby and exited the hospital. His words made me well up with emotion and I had to compose myself to go on doing my Santa duties without breaking down. It made me realize the simple act of putting on the suit and giving of myself to portray Santa Claus for a couple of hours really did have a much deeper meaning and emotional connection to patients and families this time of year. I forgot about anything that concerned me and my work getting done on time and shifted my focus on just being Santa Claus for all who came into the building. This is no way me bragging about what I have done but I hope a story that might perhaps make you give of your time also.

The simple act of embodying this Christmas icon that has brought people so much joy and filled their memories with happy moments throughout their lifetime. It takes them right back to childhood and then growing up and embracing the magic and storytelling. It's going on my fifth Christmas season that I play Santa for the hospital that I work at and the encounters with the patients and family members is what keeps me doing it. From cell phone messages to patients' children, handing out candy canes or just giving out hugs it is extremely special to me.

One of the best gifts you can give is the gift of giving of yourself. When you do things that won't bring you any monetary value and it's out of service and in the spirit of giving. Then you truly embody the spirit of the season and Saint Nicholas. The quote of Mahatma Gandhi comes to mind "the best way to find yourself is to lose yourself in the service of others". Also, the quote from Robert Louis Stevenson "Don't judge each day by the harvest you reap, but by the seeds you plant." Lao-tzu the Chinese philosopher and author of the Tao Te Ching said, "The master can keep giving because there is no end to his wealth." If you can't offer money to those who are less fortunate, say a silent blessing for them. Look for opportunities to fill the empty spaces in other people's lives with loving energy in the form of kindness, compassion, joy, and forgiveness.

Yuletide Family Recipes

WANS

5 lb flour
¾ qt. milk
2 sticks butter
2 cups sugar
5 tsp. baking powder
1 tsp salt
5 eggs
3 tbsp of anise extract

Heat milk. Remove from heat. Melt in butter. Add sugar, eggs, salt. Beat well. Add anise extract. Add flour w/wire whisk. When the mixture gets doughy, put flour on the table and knead until it isn't sticky. Cut into chunks. Roll chunks through pasta machine (or Kitchenaid mixer with pasta attachment) first on wide setting, then on thin setting. Cut into strips with pastry wheel. Twirl the strips into a "fairy's wand" or "rosette". Deep fry until brown. Coat w/honey and sprinkles or powdered sugar.

From the kitchen of: _____
Recipe for: Russian Coffee Cake 1 hr. 15 min.
Ingredients: _____ (Mix topping set aside)
350°

4 cups flour   — Topping —
2 sticks butter   ½ cup sugar
4 tsp. Vanilla   ½ cup Walnuts Chopped
1 tsp. Baking Powder 1 tsp. Cinnamon
1 Pt. Sour Cream
2 cups Sugar
4 EGGS
2 tsp. Baking Soda
½ tsp. SALT

Sweet Potato Muffins

400° F
1¼ cups sugar
1¼ cups mashed sweet potatoes
2 eggs
1 tsp cinnamon
½ tsp nutmeg
¼ tsp salt
1 cup milk
1½ cups flour
1 stick butter
2 tsp baking powder

① Mix potatoes, butter + sugar until smooth. Add eggs.
② Add dry ingredients. Alternate with milk.
③ Grease tins well. Fill tins to the top. Bake 25-30 minutes.

Classic Pizzelles
6 eggs
3½ cups flour
1½ cups sugar
2 Tbsp. vanilla or anise

1 cup margarine, melted (do not use more or substitute oil)
4 tsp. baking powder

Beat eggs, adding sugar gradually. Beat until smooth.
Add cooled margarine and vanilla or anise.
Sift flour and baking powder.
Blend into egg mixture until smooth. Dough will be sticky, enough to be dropped by spoon.
Bake in Pizzelle Baker. Makes approximately 60 pizzelles.
VARIATION: PIZZELLES WITH NUTS. Finely chop one cup of walnuts or pecans. Blend into Classic Pizzelle dough.

Chocolate Pizzelles
½ cup cocoa
½ cup sugar
½ tsp. baking powder

Sift cocoa, additional sugar and baking powder into dry ingredients for Classic Pizzelles.
Blend into egg mixture until smooth. Makes approximatley 60 chocolate pizzelles.
Serving Hint: Pizzelles provide the base for a delicious ice cream sandwich. Can also be rolled and filled with desired fillings for a perfect dessert.

AFTERWORD

Today's version of Yuletide has changed over time but still represents a harmonious fusion of historical pagan roots and Christian celebrations. We have explored the folklore and imagery of the holiday season. The connection we have to traditions passed down from our ancestors and rituals that make this time of year magical and special. Most of all my intention for this book was to share the medium's perspective on what spirit shares about the holiday season. For anyone mourning the loss of a loved one or going through the grief process, perhaps this book could offer a little light to the darkness. Through the personal stories shared from mediumship readings and messages from our spirit communicators, we could find that our loved ones are truly only a thought away. We also gain a greater perspective on the power of consciousness and how that links us to the spirit world. We are all spiritual beings having a human experience and will always be connected through soul consciousness.

As we come together to celebrate, we remember and honor those that went before us. We live and carry on their legacy and dreams, those we lost are still with us and were not their physical bodies. The only thing that ceases is the physical, the light that made our loved ones who they were in life still shines bright today. They are at the dinner table, baking, caroling and always ever so near. We need only to think about or mention them and that sacred connection is made. The spirit world is not a faraway place, it's around everyone and everything. It's attainable for everyone to reach and everyone can do it. We are all souls and have the same hardware, we just need to have the confidence and knowledge on how to use it. Be open to the signs and the subtle ways spirit communicates and lets us know that they are near.

Celebrate the returning of the light and your ancestral connection by honoring those that went before us. This is the time for remembrance and to embrace one another and get through the darkness of the Yule. I wish you the Merriest of Yuletides and a winter solstice that brings you happiness and positive transformation in the new year.

About the Author

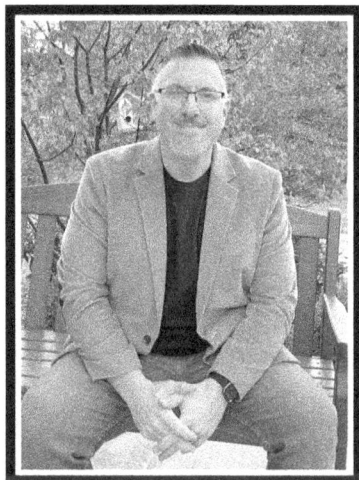

Richard lives in Rockaway Township, New Jersey with his wife and three children. He has many events and appearances to offer the public a chance to experience spirit art mediumship and to offer proof of the continuity of life. He also offers private in person and virtual readings for anyone interested. When not doing psychic mediumship, Richard investigates many paranormal cases and locations. He has authored many books on the supernatural that have received critical acclaim. He also teaches, lectures and provides seminars on various paranormal topics. When not working he enjoys the outdoors and connecting with nature and of course his love of fishing.

ALSO BY RICHARD MOSCHELLA

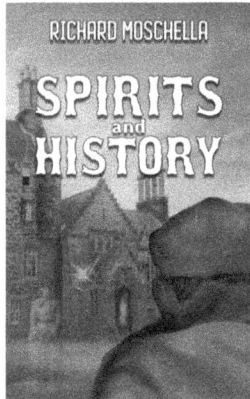

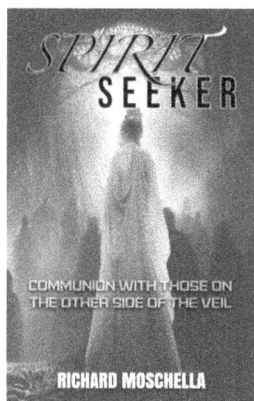

SPIRIT SEEKER

COMMUNION WITH THOSE ON
THE OTHER SIDE OF THE VEIL

RICHARD MOSCHELLA

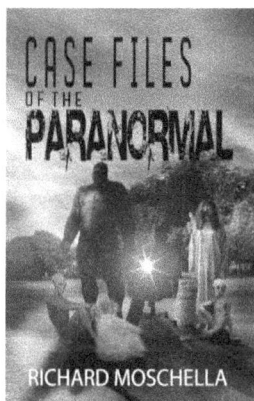

CASE FILES OF THE PARANORMAL

RICHARD MOSCHELLA

SPIRIT VOICES

RICHARD MOSCHELLA